Weaving Of Worlds: a Day on Île d'Yeu

Greg Lockhart

Greg Lockhart is intrigued by the threads of history and memory that draw friends, communities, and nations together. He is aware that these fine strings can fray and fail. A former soldier, his books show that he knows better than most Australian historians about the conduct and the terrible costs of war. As a student of modern Vietnamese history, he studied archival holdings in Paris. His compelling account of a visit to Île d'Yeu, just off the coast of western France, is at once a good story and a brilliant example of the arts of learning, listening and patient observation.

David Walker AM, Honorary Professorial Fellow, Asia Institute, University of Melbourne, and author of Anxious Nation *(1999) and* Stranded Nation (2019)

Journeys into the past are both a weaving and an unweaving of threads; a remembering and a forgetting; history and memory in unending argument with each another. Ego-histoire, the construction of a personal version, might be a way out of that dilemma. In *Weaving of Worlds*, Greg Lockhart picks up the traces of his and others lives in France, Australia, Vietnam and elsewhere, and makes of them a ravelling and unravelling pattern. Ultimately about the strangeness of war, and what it makes people do, this is an affective and effective essay, complex and moving, paradoxical and illuminating.

Martin Edmond, author of Chronicle of the Unsung (2004), Luca Antara: passages in search of Australia (2006), Battarbee and Namatjira (2014), Isinglass (2019) *and others*

Greg Lockhart was a Captain in the Australian Army in Vietnam. A distinguished military historian, he has written over twenty articles for *Pearls & Irritations*. His acclaimed books include *The Minefield* (2007). Now, *Weaving of Worlds* is a delightful story of his one-day visit to Île d'Yeu with his wife, Monique in 2012. For those of us who can't travel these days, this is a colourful and refreshing story that weaves together narratives of history, travel, and people.

Ile d'Yeu is a windswept French-Atlantic Island that has been washed over by Vikings, missionaries, the French, the English, the Germans and more. I should have recalled that it was the burial place of Marshal Petain, the hero of Verdun and the villain of Vichy France. Beyond the political and military history of the island is an intimate story of the weaving of relationships of family and friends and of how all individuals are linked in history. "If one member suffers, all suffer together with it; if one member is honoured, all rejoice with it."

A challenging and enjoyable read.

> *John Menadue AO, Distinguished Public Servant, Former Ambassador to Japan, Chief Executive Officer of Qantas, author of* Things you learn along the way *(1999), and Founder and Editor of* Pearls and Irritations.

Weaving of Worlds: a Day on Île d'Yeu
Greg Lockhart

First published by Reading Sideways Press,
March 2023

Leiden, The Netherlands
readingsidewayspress.com
readingsidewayspress@gmail.com

This book is copyright. The copyright of the original text belongs to Greg Lockhart. Except for private study, research, criticism or reviews, as permitted under the Copyright Act, no part of this book may be reproduced, stored in a retrieval system or transmitted in any form or by any means without prior written permission. Enquiries should be made to the publisher.

Typeset in Avara and Caudex

ISBN 978-0-64547225-1-6

Designed by Amarawati Ayuningtyas
Proofreading by Michele Fuller
All photos are by the author except for where otherwise stated.

*For Dominique and Dominique Turbé
And in Memory of Maurice Esseul,
1928-2021*

The Magic of Islands

Islands have always exerted a powerful attraction on our imagination. To go to an island is to enter an unknown world, a fabulous, inaccessible world, often populated by epic tales that cradle our childhood; a place where the ocean is the only master.

The one whose history is being told to you is the island of Yeu, vigilant guardian of the Vendée coast. In the mists of time, the elements have shaped its outline. Light and refuge above the waters, against winds and tides, it has endured over the ages, time and again, the fury of the raging waves and the covetousness of invaders.

> Maurice Esseul, *Petite histoire de l'île d'Yeu* (*A Short History of Île d'Yeu*)

Self-consciousness emerges under the sign of that which has already happened, as the fulfillment of something always already begun. We speak so much of memory because there is so little of it left.

> Pierre Nora, 'Between Memory and History: Les Lieux de Mémoire,' translated by Marc Roudebush, *Representations*.

Contents

Prologue	1
I	7
II	12
III	39
IV	69
V	82
VI	97
VII	106
Acknowledgements	111
Bibliography	128

Prologue

One day in 2012, I visited Île d'Yeu off the west coast of France and wrote this book soon after. I put the manuscript aside for nine years. Then, counterintuitively in the time of Covid-19 lockdowns, it occurred to me that there might be interest in a story that was as much about travel as it was a personal memoir and in histories that radiated from the island.

Shortly before this manuscript was finished, another piece of travel writing about the island, the only one I know about apart from mine, came serendipitously to my attention. This is a playful three-page travel romance republished twice in *The New Yorker* on 28th June and 13th October 2021 after its original publication in that journal on 5th August 1939. By Ludwig Bemelmans, an American writer and illustrator of children's stories, particularly the famous *Madeline* series, the article is called 'The Isle of God'. Suddenly, across 82 years and on the other side the world, I felt the Bemelmans story floating mine.

The Ile d'Yeu is immediately beautiful and at once familiar, he wrote, as if drawing on a childhood dream. *Its round, small harbor is stuffed with boats; the fat tuna schooners lie in the centre, around them sleek sardine and lobster boats.* The first house he came to from the dock at Port Joinville *is a poem of a hotel,* with tangerine velvet *fauteuils,* armchairs, and *tout confort moderne,* meaning hot and cold water and central heating. Outside, overlooking the harbor and under an awning behind some yew trees, are the *apéritif* tables and chairs.

The name of another hotel, Hotel Turbé, whose cooking he recommends, is close to the heart of my story. We will see that Turbé is a well-known family name on the island, and central to the knot of relations that make this story.

There is much else in the Bemelmans romance I did not see, as it was set in another time. Still, I believe it. *The sardine is the banana of the Ile-d'Yeu,* says Bemelemans. *You slip and fall on sardines every-*

where. They look out of the small market baskets that les vieux corbeaux – old crows, the local expression meaning old women dressed in black – *carry home. Sardine tails stick out of fishermen's pockets, they are dragged past you in barrels. Other, larger fish, the tuna predominantly, wander by hung over the shoulders of strong sailors, or tied to bicycles, or pushed along in carts.*

Also from another time were the *sailors, with every shade of color in their sensible pants and blouses a hundred times patched.* And there was the three-hour walk from Port Joinville to the rock-rimmed Port de la Meule on the southern coast of the island, which brings one, in the Bemelmans story, to the *Auberge des Homardiers*, a tavern specialising in lobster dishes.

Though still handled playfully, the romance has something of a dark lining towards the end. Late in World War One, we are told, an American submarine had limped into La Meule on a crippled engine. Apparently, while waiting some weeks for spare parts to fix the engine, a member of the crew had a romance with one Madame Pompano, who owned the *auberge*. The crewman was Swanky Franky, who promised her the world – *a little house in Engle-*

wood, New Jersey ... electric irons, a vacuum cleaner, and even a voiture Buick. But when the submarine was repaired, Franky slipped out of the harbour and went silently to sea in the vessel. So it was, Bemelmans warned tourists, with a play on the lobster dish *cooked in the American way,* if on entering the *Auberge des Homardiers* you are asked whether you are American, you'd best say you are a *Scot or Australian.*

As it happens, my *Australian* narrative of Île d'Yeu will include other fateful wartime themes; one picking up on the presence of German submarines around the island in 1917, another relating to dramatic events around La Meule in 1942; yet another revolves around the exile of Marshal Pétain on the island from 1945. While the Bemelmans story floats mine, I think, mine carries his into another time – history.

And history is full of surprises. Bemelmans tells us he found a fisherman's house for a three-months stay at *the holiest address in this world,* Number 3, Rue du Paradis, Saint-Sauveur, Île d'Yeu. He could not have known, however, that within one month of the original 5th August 1939 publication of his story, on 1 September the Germans would invade Poland. After that, my hunch is he did not stay long.

Still, I will share in 2012 and beyond his dream of 'The Isle of God'. All those years ago, he had heard in the local store, Les Nouvelles Galleries Insulaires, something we'd all like to believe. Since *d'Yeu* is an ancient distortion of the French term *Dieu,* God, he was told, *Île d'Yeu* is really *Île de Dieu,* Isle of God.

The island's historian, Maurice Esseul, reverses that story. *Yeu* is derived from the Old Norse term *Oya,* signifying from pre-Christian times *land with a watery nimbus, the small isle,* (and used as a suffix in the names of over 145 Norwegian islands). After the 500s, when Christian missionaries reached Île d'Yeu, some monastic charts used the Latin term *insula,* meaning island, to name the island *Insula Oya.* This went on until the 1300s. From the 1400s to the mid-1800s, the name *isle Dieu* did appear on maps. But then, of course, the opposite of what Bemelmans heard was true: the term *isle Dieu,* Isle of God, was *a phonetic distortion of Île d'Yeu* – which became, in the second half of the 1800s, the definitive name of the island on all geographic and administrative documents.

Now, off the coast of the Vendée in the Bay of

Biscay, those documents place Île d'Yeu in the region of France known as Pays de la Loire.

I

The ferry crossing from Fromentine, on the Bay of Biscay, to Île d'Yeu is unfamiliar to me, and yet the island's coastline appears as if it were a remembered shore. Halfway into the eleven-nautical-mile passage through a lazy swell, a faint blur smudges the horizon. In the wind, sea gulls sway and swoop. The blur stretches slowly into a black line that rises between sky and water to embody the reddish-brown, rocky shelf of the island's east coast.

I am visiting France from Australia this European summer with my wife Monique. Dominique Turbé and his wife also named Dominique Turbé, née Deschamps, whom we have known for many years, now live in the village of Le Temple de Bretagne near Nantes. We are visiting them from Paris with Monique's sister Edith. I suggested a day excursion to the island. Dominique has family links with the old fishing community on the island, and I am mildly curious about the place to which, in 1945, the French state exiled Marshal Pétain, the former President of the Vichy Regime.

The ferry rounds the breakwater and enters the harbour at the capital Port Joinville. A white fleet sits in the water, and, around the harbour, white-washed stone buildings stand in an arc that is centered on *la mairie* where the French tri-colour hangs on a pole angled high above the entrance. We disembark and the eye adjusts on a hazy morning to the confined space in the port and registers the bands and blocks of colour on the white surfaces of the boats and buildings.

We buy baguettes and some *tartes aux fruits* to take away for lunch. Dominique hires a small jeep with a canvas top and open sides to drive us around the island. Then, suddenly, the sky darkens: there is an Atlantic squall.

In winter ferocious gales drive mountainous waves onto the island's west coast and shroud its narrow surface in freezing fogs and mists. On the eastern side, tides surge through the channel between the coast and the continent. My other companion on this trip is Monsieur Maurice Esseul's book, *Petite histoire de l'île d'Yeu*, just out this year. It recounts how, in February 1904, tidal waves breached the breakwater, swept away the quays and inundated the houses around the harbour, causing havoc from which it took the port a year to recover.

By contrast, our summer squall blows over in twenty minutes. After this wet scrubbing, the sky is cobalt blue. Like a second sun, the port's white surfaces become a single, lustrous source of light. And now in dazzling luminosity, the bright colours painted on the gunwales, inboards and wheelhouses of the boats dance with the bright colours on the doors, window frames and shutters of the buildings: shades of blue, green, turquoise, yellow, lime-yellow, red, orange, brown and grey. The tiled rooftops are the colour of soft clay.

We get in the jeep and drive through the area behind the waterfront. The white houses are so perfectly adjoined on either side of the narrow streets that, despite their colourful doors and window shutters, they present the same inscrutable front to the world as rows of cabins on an ocean liner. Before long we come out of this tight-knit neighbourhood and stop at a freestanding house with front and back gardens with fruit trees.

Dominique's brother-in-law Daniel, who was married to Dominique's now deceased sister Sophie, invites us inside. We are offered a glass of white wine and chat about Australia, its population, size, and climates. We talk about ourselves and are complimented on our French.

I say that I went to the Vietnam War and, later, became an historian of it. During various visits to France to research the period of the so-called First Indochina War (1945-54), I've learned limited French, can read for my purposes, and spoke clearly today. Monique and Edith tell a different story: Monique's primary education was in Vietnamese and Edith's in French, and both completed the seven years of their secondary education in French at the Lycée Yersin among the pine trees at Dalat in the southern highlands of Vietnam.

In February 1975, Monique left Vietnam when she received a scholarship to further her teaching career at the University of Sydney. She remained in Australia when Saigon fell two months later and went on to complete a Master of Education Degree. Edith left Vietnam with her children in a small boat a few years later. A hazardous voyage to Malaysia, which included attacks by Thai pirates, led her to a refugee camp. There, on finding she had been a teacher of French, doctors from Médecins Sans Frontières, employed her as a translator and fast-tracked her passage to Paris, where she has now, in 2012, lived for over 30 years.

Dominique and Dominique raise some family matters. Then, with our stories in various states of telling, Daniel says something unexpected that will tilt the history of Île d'Yeu into the shadows of my own past and push both into the future: *je pense que quelques Australiens sont enterrés dans le cimetière*, I think some Australians are buried in the cemetery. No one knows who they were; Dominique says we will visit the graves later in the day. We wave goodbye to our host and drive off to circumnavigate the island, which is nine and a half kilometres long and four kilometres at its widest point.

II

We stop at La Pointe du But, Target Point, a rocky promontory on the north coast to eat our baguettes in the lee of an abandoned stone building. It seems to have been a foghorn station related to an older version of the beacon-tower, freshly painted yellow and grey, which stands on a reef a few hundred metres out to sea.

This is a treacherous stretch of water, says Dominique, and, as I wonder how the tower was erected in such a place, he recalls, with deep respect for both the wisdom of his forebears and the dangers of the sea, how he was warned as a boy never to go out into the waters off this point alone.

Dominique's stories also stir memories of war. In January 1917, he says seriously, while still looking out to sea, the Norwegian ship *Ymer* was torpedoed by a German submarine off the coast, and a party of twelve sailors from the island lived up to its sea-faring traditions by ignoring the danger and the freezing conditions and attempting to save the survivors on the wreck in a rescue boat. He says the rescue ran into serious difficulties. Unable to return to the island, rescuers and survivors alike were carried off by the tides and landed three days later, on the tiny isle off Raguénès, south of Concarneau.

Monsieur Esseul writes in *Petite histoire* that Île d'Yeu's population of about 4,000 people *followed with anguish the news from the front* and, also that, alas, *the rhythm of the tides and the ringing of church bells more frequently announced mourning than joyful events*: the rescue mission cost the island community dearly. Six of the twelve sailors, including one Emmanuel Turbé, perished, leaving 21 orphans on the island. Five of the seven Norwegians who were taken off the wreck did not survive either.

For Dominique, the rescue still raises a riddle of identity: his relationship with Emmanuel Turbé. Apparently, Dominique's grandfather Joseph Turbé had an older brother named Emmanuel who was

30 in 1917. Yet Dominique's aunt thinks that he was probably not the Emmanuel involved in the rescue; that the Emmanuel thus involved was a namesake of Joseph's brother. If so, this would mean that the hero, *un vrai marin*, was not directly related to Dominique's family and must have come from another branch of the Île d'Yeu Turbé line.

Petite histoire notes that the Kingdom of Norway erected a monument to the lost heroes in 1922, which still stands in a small square at Port Joinville. National wreath laying ceremonies are held there, and, after local weddings, the wedding parties visit the monument and circle it, singing local folksongs.

While Dominique is talking, I look over a swathe of tall grass that is bending in the wind. My eyes come to rest on a circular stone structure that stands just above ground level on a small rise not far behind us. The structure is related to a network of stone foundations on which other structures once stood. Dominique says that it is the vestige of a German military fortification, perhaps a blockhouse gun emplacement such as those that commonly exist in more ample and alien form on continental France. Nearby there is another old position called the *Machine Gun Post*. Dominique goes on wryly to inform me that in recent years real estate agents have been advertising bunkers as fashionable property options for people with a taste for military architecture. However, this Île d'Yeu instance of the art is unlikely to be refurbished and reoccupied. It is too much a stub of its original construction, which had been small to begin with. Especially in winter, this windswept northern promontory would be a very isolated site. In any case, community zoning laws preclude building in the area. But here it remains, a bare remnant of a dark time, as Dominique begins to recount that, as a boy, his father lived through the German occupation of the island during World War Two.

This story, which is foreshadowed in our friendship, makes me think back to an exchange of gifts that took place after we arrived in Le Temple two nights ago.

When Monique left Vietnam to study in Australia in February 1975, she carried some exquisitely hand-embroidered items of white linen to present as gifts: tablecloths, table pieces and serviettes, embossed with red roses, pink roses, and peach blossoms. This linen would have been stored away when, in 1978, we met the Dominiques at The Maples, a weatherboard apartment block for married students set amid maple and liquid amber trees at Sydney University. They were involved in post-graduate commercial studies, after which they returned to France. The French involvement in Indochina, Monique's secondary education in French, and my PhD in modern Vietnamese history, which meant reading French as well as Vietnamese books were, I think, parts of whatever created the friendship that has caused us so inevitably to re-gather its threads each time we have visited France.

Over half a lifetime, Monique gradually gave her pile of linen away, so that, as we prepared for this trip, she felt moved to give them her last pieces, a table piece and two serviettes embroidered with pink roses. There was something else; a lapel pin, which featured a gold-rimmed opal continent of Australia with a gold kangaroo jumping across it. The pin was packed in a small brown suede box with a gold spring-hinge that snapped crisply open and shut. Monique bought this to give to her father, knowing he would be proud to show it off on his lapel. But as she said, as she packed the small suede box to take to France, Saigon fell, and she never saw her father again.

When she presented these gifts, Dominique's response showed the importance he attached to them. He and I had been discussing the work of the French aviator and writer Antoine de Saint-Exupéry, his great 1931 novel *Vol de nuit* and his 1942 story *Pilote de guerre*. I was saying how remarkable it was that in *Pilote de guerre* Saint-Exupéry had woven a meditation on the nation, civilisation, and humanity around an account of his dangerous surveillance mission of German forces during the battle for France in May 1940. *Pilote de guerre* was the work in which he observed from a great height the disintegration of the French nation. As he flew over the refugees fleeing the German army's blitzkrieg, they looked like *interminable black syrup* trickling down the roads. This was also the book in which he went on to ponder the *responsible*, inherently *loving* relations that would be necessary to revivify the nation and rescue 40 million French people from the darkness into which they had been plunged. Moved by Monique's gifts, Dominique presented me with his father's own marked and annotated copy of Saint-Exupéry's *Pilote de guerre*. The book is Number 705 of the 109th *edition*, which came off the press on 25th November 1947.

Such is the weaving of worlds.

From June 1940, when a small German detachment occupied the island, to August 1944, when Canadian warships liberated it, Dominique continues, as we walk around the stump of the old fortification, his grandmother had to raise his father Claude Turbé and eight of his brothers and sisters, nine children altogether. Dominique's grandfather Joseph, who had been with the French Navy at the Dardanelles in Turkey during World War One, was too old to be in the second one, and so remained on the island. Life there was seriously restricted by a severance of contacts with the mainland and an oppressive Nazi regime of curfews, surveillance, and other restrictions, including the strict prohibition on the fishing fleet taking to sea, a measure that created conditions of near starvation.

Joseph supported his large family by evading the Nazi restrictions on fishing. He would go out to sea in his small dinghy and smuggle the catch ashore. The family lived mainly on fish and garden vegetables. Dominique said: *j'ai toujours entendu mon père dire qu'il avait eu faim*, I always heard my father say he had been hungry.

Claude Turbé has left traces of his experience of that time and of the thirst for existence it gave him. I was vaguely aware of this after Dominique passed his father's copy of *Pilote de guerre* on to me at Le Temple. Claude had bought it from the Beaufreton Bookshop – which only recently went out of business – in the neo-classical Passage Pommeraye in Nantes. He had read this copy as a young man, around 1951 or 1952, searching for clues about life. He had marked numerous passages in it. The marks had been made in pencil – both vertical lines in the margins and underlines in the text.

A phrase jumped out: *le droit d'être*, the right to be. These words come late in the story where Saint-Exupéry, after shaking off some German fighters by flying into the sun has completed his dangerous surveillance mission around Arras in northern France and made it back to base. Now, drained, he feels that survival has conferred on him a somewhat greater, unspoken right to commune with his comrades, both living and departed: his sense of the right to be signifies a heightened sense of having escaped extinction.

This thought comes back to me in the silences of Dominique's narrative: the passages his father marked in *Pilote de guerre* make me feel sure that he had read Saint-Exupéry's wartime work through the lens of his childhood experience of the German occupation.

Pilote de guerre presents a highly mechanistic account of the defeat of France, hinged by the Cartesian notion of god *l'horloger*, the watchmaker or supreme creator. The first chapter explains that, with villages abandoned and the roadside ditches clogged with vehicles of all descriptions – most bizarrely, the agricultural ones – *a summer has gone wrong, all the clocks are broken* on the churches and stations and in the houses. The world has gone haywire; *god has retired from it*. If one of the last phrases Claude underlined in the book was the right to be, one of the earliest is the conclusion to the passage on broken clocks: *Et l'on meurt en été*, And one dies in summer.

The northern summer had of course caught Île d'Yeu in the disastrous sweep of continental events. After German forces, including General Rommel's Panzer Division pushed virtually unopposed towards Brittany on 17th June 1940, that very afternoon Marshal Pétain was elected head of the French government in Bordeaux with a mandate to negotiate an armistice. The Breton coast and its offshore islands, which had a fiercely independent seagoing tradition, were central to German Atlantic strategy; the first German delegation arrived by warship at Port Joinville to dictate to the mayor the initial conditions of the occupation on 20th June.

The people on Île d'Yeu did not experience the dislocation of the vast refugee exodus on the continent; there was nowhere for them to flee. But with the watchmaker gone and his mechanism in chaos, with the big wheels of the German juggernaut smashing into the loose cogs and weak springs of French defences, the changed expressions and behaviours of grown-ups had to convey to children the fear and confusion of defeat. And so, I think, the uncertainties of survival in a conquered community, the ambiguities of defiance and *attentisme,* the beautifully concise French term for waiting and seeing, and the fevers and depressions that consumed minds and bodies all ran into the dark lead line of Claude's pencil when he underlined the phrase And one dies in summer.

I forget the exact sequence of vertically marked

passages and horizontally underlined phrases that Claude went on to mark with his pencil between that unseasonal death rattle and the resounding <u>right to be</u>. But his pencil generally scored text that represented Saint-Exupéry's idea of a civilized community and nation with its source in a Christian sense of god's love unifying individuals in the body of Christ. The authority would be 1 Corinthians 12: *If one member suffers, all suffer together with it; if one member is honored, all rejoice together with it.*

Underscoring the inseparable grand themes of love and death, Claude Turbé's line is readily recalled from my copy of *Pilote de guerre*. <u>Defeat divides, victory is the fruit of love</u>; sacrifice is not a parody, a suicide, it is the responsible giving of an individual to the collective; <u>it is beautiful to sacrifice oneself</u>. True love (of country as of other beings) is tacit, it is the <u>network of relations in which we are fulfilled</u>. <u>Man is only a knot of relations; the right to be</u> is the right to be related, to be more than oneself.

Finally: <u>victory alone ties the knot; each one of us is responsible for all</u>. The conquered must be silent. But resistance germinating in acts of unspoken love would reconstitute the fallen nation, the broken civilisation, and the lost sense of humanity in <u>the victory to come</u>.

***

Perhaps such a victory has come; there is something eternal about the glorious summer afternoon into which we drive around the coast in the area, known locally as *Les Broches*. Small fishermen's cabins sometimes appear. Two we pass are pure white, with bright rooftops, one painted red, one orange, standing on an olive mound beneath a powdery blue sky.

Intensified in the purity of the light, the shapes and colours of modern abstraction – Mondrian's – come to mind. The sea is a maze of saucer-shaped agitations, much as Monet depicted it over a century ago at Belle-Île, another Biscay-island 30 or 40 kilometres to the north. Monet's purplish and greenish blue water is close to what I see, although the tall cliffs and towering rock piles and arches that stand in his seascapes at Belle-Île are not a part of the scenery on Île d'Yeu. Here, the lower cliffs and flatter rock formations, which extend into an apron of submerged reefs off the west coast, are less spectacular – and maybe why Île d'Yeu never supported a colony of impressionist painters, as Belle-Île did when Monet and his Australian associate John Peter Russell resided there.

About a third of the way down the coast we get out of the jeep to walk across some small hills and around some inlets. The earth is as hard as granite. It is cut back by wind and rain and bound by short grasses and wild shrubs. The light is not only pure because there is no pollution: there is no dust. I help Edith up a steep embankment. Dominique says that *Oya* – the same *Oya* in *Insula Oya*, the name given to the island on ancient charts of Viking origin – is the name of a flower. She says that this is the flower whose root systems spread in the small dunes around beaches. Other wildflowers, delicate white, yellow, pink, and mauve speckle the fields and grow in tufts of greenery in the crevices of the low cliffs.

We look back across a small beach to La Croix du Châtelet standing on a promontory. As though beaming holy light through a tempest, The Cross is mounted like a mast in a sculptured ship symbolising the arrival of the first missionaries from across the sea. Perhaps they landed on that beach over which The Cross now looks down.

Disciples of Saint Columba originally brought Christianity to Île d'Yeu. They had established a monastery on the island before 600. This establishment was destroyed by Sarrasin and Viking invasions soon after 800. A second monastery called Saint-Étienne was established inland to the east of here before 1000. Not long after that, the monks, whose religious works included the cultivation of the fields and the education of the young, had the resources to build the church of Saint Sauveur, which has now been the centre of the island's single parish for almost a thousand years.

Today, 30 or 40 people, many of them children, sit and play on the beach with small boats and canoes piled up nearby, brightly coloured in the local fashion. The beach is itself marked off from the road by low picket and railing fences. Most of the people group themselves in a loose knot around one spot on the sand. As in France generally, the beach is a public space on Île d'Yeu. Yet that grouping and the association one feels it has with the white huts huddled around the car park, huts that suggest an outpost of the island's two main agglomerations at Port Joinville and Saint Sauveur, seem to hint at a local desire to *squat* on the beach and exclude visitors.

A reference to the island's beaches in Bemelemans 'The Isle of God' suggested a geographically imposed sense of seclusion that has nonetheless attracted outsiders. After mentioning that one of the small hotels by the dock had 26 rooms, all reserved each summer for the same French families visiting from the continent, the 1939 romance says:

> *The coast of the Ile is a succession of small private beaches, each one like a room with three walls, with curtains of rock and greenery, and a cave to dress in. Once you arrive, it's yours. On the open side is the water, its little waves washing up on fine sand. Back and forth over the green sea sails the sardine fleet, its colored sails leaning over the water.*

There are no sails today and no fine sand just ahead of us. But little waves wash up on a bay rimmed with sharp rocks, as we look across it to the most notable building on the island and a national historical monument since 1890.

In 1342, at the beginning of the Hundred Years War, the Old Château (see photo section) was built on the Port Joinville we see before us surrounded by the sea. On the landward side, the only access is via a drawbridge crossing the chasm of a seawater moat. During the twenty minutes it takes for us

to walk around the bay I become briefly aware of
a light plane flying overhead. It must be *en route*
from the continent to the island.

A Tourist Office sign that stands at the head of the
drawbridge explains to visitors that the fortress
is an example of *château-cour* architecture in its
most highly developed form. Inside the battle-
ments, which are many feet thick, and which must
have been an exceedingly cold and gloomy source
of security in winter – although winter was no
season for invaders – the courtyard contained a
bakery, cookhouse, blacksmith's forge, and accom-
modation for the defenders. Thus, for three centuries, the governors of the island lived.

We don't cross the bridge. Even though the sign
says the Old Château is open for inspection, the
front door is closed, and we are the only ones
around.

This was not the case on the day in 1355 when
an English armada encircled the island flying the
colours of the Black Prince. An illuminated illustration I remember seeing reproduced in Simon
Schama's *A History of Britain* (2000) suggests what
the defenders were up against. The illustration is
from Froissart's *Chronicles* (1460-80) and it shows

an English army with the Black Prince on its way to France. The pale blue sky suggests summer. A herald is trumpeting the arrival of the force from the forecastle of the front ship. Above him, the blood Red Cross of St George standing out against the backdrop of a pure white flag is flying. With a few figures revealing red tunics through chinks in their armor, the troops stand on the ships in dense clusters resembling a metallic mass of black beetles or massed samurai in a Kurosawa film.

Such was the army led by the celebrated Captain Robert Knowles that landed on Île d'Yeu – most likely across the open east coast beaches, rather than across the dangerous west coast reefs. Apparently, a small garrison fled in the face of the alien array.

Why, I wonder, am I feeling strangely at home in this story? Because the sky is blue today? Because I too was a Captain in another war in another place and time? Because that Red Cross of St George still provided the strong red vertical and horizontal axes of the British Union Jack that, with its adoption in 1801, framed the political-cultural narrative of my ancestry and, indeed, my career?

Centering that Red Cross, the Union Jack flew over

the long white settler conquest of Australasia, as the British Army's *red coats* secured it in the nineteenth century. Again, featuring that Red Cross, the Union Jack was retained in the top flagstaff corner of the flag that was used from 1901 and flew 70 years later over my own involvement in the Vietnam War. Are there not, then, fundamental reasons why a detail from Monsieur Esseul's *Petite histoire* was always going to jump out at me? The islanders still tell how, in the 37-year interval between 1355, when the English occupied Île d'Yeu, and 1392 when Clisson, a Constable of France, reconquered it, their ancestors were oppressed by *les hommes rouges*, the so-called red men, because *red was the colour of their coats.*

Must we not subjectify history, because our narratives of it represent our experience of remotely remembered things? Does not memory mirror history and make it a remote imitation of self and the self a remote imitation of it? Might not memory generate self?

The invasions continued down the centuries, particularly in the sixteenth century it seems, and no two were the same. In 1550, two or three thousand Spaniards who had been fighting in northern

France easily doubled the island's population when they plundered it on their way home. They laid siege to the Château and left after its defenders held out for several weeks. English Admiral Montgomery let loose another force of naval ruffians to loot the island in 1573; the list of depredations goes on.

By the middle of the next century, however, the Age of Reason – and of its seminal mathematician and philosopher René Descartes (1595-1650) – had led to the application of rational and scientific methods to military as well as social problems. Advances in artillery that went with the greater effectiveness of Vauban style fortresses (to protect the vulnerable east coast) meant that the Château's defences had become obsolete. In 1657, the governor moved his capital to Saint Sauveur and the Château slipped into the past.

***

We walk back to the jeep, aware of the hard, pared back beauty of the hills in the flame of summer. When Dominique asks me if I can see why he and Dominique want to live on the island, I have no hesitation saying *yes*. This is a place that yields little surplus. But in the dry warmth of the sun its spare surface makes me feel close to the miracle of existence.

Life on Île d'Yeu is tenacious. In ancient times, the island supported conifer and oak forests. But with its clearing in recent centuries, firewood has often been scarce, the main fuel substitute being cakes made of straw mixed into cow dung and dried in the sun. The wheat crop usually served the population's needs and kept four or five mills turning. The vineyards produced palatable wine. In good years, there were oats for several hundred head of cattle and grass for a few thousand sheep. Horses were tiny – like Shetland ponies. Fish always supplemented the diet. Monsieur Esseul's description of the *egalitarian* character of the people relates well to the shared labours and face-to-face relations that regulated life in a small community.

The island's outlook is as irreducibly global as local. Monsieur Esseul emphasises that from the time of Charlemagne, kings have made the islanders beneficiaries of royal tax exemptions to compensate them for the frequent losses they suffered at the hands of raiders and invaders.

From at least 1400, when Île d'Yeu's main port (now Port Joinville) was named Port Breton, the island has been integrated into the Breton coastal trade in salt, wheat, and wine. A few decades after the Portuguese rounded the Cape of southern Africa and reached India in 1498, Île d'Yeu's ships began fishing for white tuna far out in the Atlantic and, quite likely, off the west coast of Africa. (Which reminds me of a startling suggestion Dominique made about the possible diffusion of the Turbé family name from Île d'Yeu: she told me that, when one of their daughters was teaching French in Senegal a few years ago, she discovered a public square in Dakar called Place Turbé.)

By the 1700s, Île d'Yeu tuna-fleets, which were away between May and September, are known to have contained a dozen boats: women worked the fields. In the same century, British corsairs sailing out of Guernsey and Jersey periodically plundered shipping along the Breton coast, cut communications with the continent, and seriously constrained the island's economy. Still, island notables in league with entrepreneurs and money

from the slave traders in Nantes[1] made fortunes in
the 1770s and beyond by providing an offshore tax
haven that enabled a thriving clandestine com-
merce in tobacco from the Caribbean and spices
and rum from the Antilles. Although not unrelated
to slavery, an *independent* as well as an *egalitarian*
spirit suffuses Île d'Yeu history.

Our next stop is the island's second port, the small
west coast one at La Meule – near where a street
in the local village is still called *Rue des Hommes
Rouges*. The port sits in a small valley oriented
east-west and turns an S-bend around a spur
jutting out into the water at right angles from the
northern side.

We stroll into the inner harbour area along a

[1.] There is a paved concourse along the riverbank in Nantes, where we walked the other day. Images of a flurry of slave ships under full sail on the Atlantic are incised on the surface of that walkway and information panels offering a history of the French slave trade are cemented into it. The panels say the trade had its appalling origins in the fifteenth century. Many other sources say the sixteenth. The trade was abolished by the Republic in 1794, reinstated by Napoleon in 1802, and definitively abolished by the Republic in 1826-9. Between about 1500 and 1829, over 4,200 slave expeditions (of one or more ships) from France sailed along a triangular route. Departing from French ports, the slavers would take people by force from colonised parts of Africa, transport them to the Caribbean and New World colonies in America, where, enslaved, their labour was of higher value because of the low cost of natural resources cultivated from the land. The products were brought back to France. This did not mean there were no slaves in France. But over 1,380,000 men, women and children were trafficked in that way. Over 1,800 slave expeditions departing from Nantes trafficked over 555,000 people in that way. Between 1763 and 1792, French slaving interests were based in Nantes, La Rochelle, Bordeaux, and Le Havre.

concourse. There are some ramshackle fishermen's huts and whitewashed buildings on the right; some small craft are sitting in the shallow water on the left. Again, there is no escaping the familiar music of bright colours that are painted on the buildings and the boats.

Someone suddenly says: *La Chapelle*, and I look around. And looking down from the top of the escarpment on the southern side of the valley is the face of the chapel at La Meule. A pale blue door complements the soft radiance of the chapel's white face, while the bell tower touches the pale blue sky at a point around which white clouds gently gather. In its striking simplicity this modest chapel is the evocation of an essential presence that reaches back before Christianity to its Celtic origins.

There is a dark side of this religiosity, which Pierre Loti suggests in his writing on Breton fishermen. His 1886 novel *Pêcheur d'Islande* is not only suffused with adoration of the Virgin, but a universal dread of death that her presence was invoked to ward off.

The work describes sorrowful statues of the Virgin being carried in processions of benediction before the fishing fleets left for Iceland in the summer and in processions of pardon after their return to port, not always with a full complement, at the time of the first mists of autumn. The legendary drunkenness of Breton fishermen then returned to re-numb their lives until the next fishing season. This afternoon, the gently glowing white face of the chapel at La Meule does not evoke the menace of death. But darkness gathers when one realises that the same monks who had built Saint Sauveur Church not long after 1000 had also built the chapel around 1030, when much church building accompanied the millennial terror that the end of the world was nigh. Even more to the point, this apocalyptic dread has never completely passed. Tourist brochures say that the chapel overlooking the port has been dedicated since 1770 to *Notre Dame de Bonnes Nouvelles*, Our Lady of Good Tidings, and the Patron of Breton fishermen.

Time is passing and we must be moving – if we are to see the Australians in the cemetery at Port Joinville – which also contains the tomb of Philippe Pétain – before the last ferry leaves for the continent.

This means a quick spin along La Route des Corbeaux, Crows' Highway, and around the southern tip of the island known as La Pointe des Corbeaux,

Crows' Point, a name that has apparently remained unchanged since the Greek geographer and historian Strabo recorded it in a text of 58 BC. A shiny pink two-horsepower Citroën passes in the opposite direction.

We stop briefly at Le Phare des Corbeaux, Crows' Lighthouse, but do not get out of the jeep. I take a photo, which manages to catch the blue door of the small white house that seems to be the entrance to the Lighthouse, together with its tall white tower and lantern painted red on top. And, in the effort it takes to look out of the side of the jeep and up to frame that lofty composition, I have a flashback to a day 30 years ago.

> *Monique and I are standing in the red lantern-top of the great whitewashed Lighthouse rising from a large keeper's complex on the point of Cape St. Vincent, near Sagres in Portugal, on the southwestern tip of Europe. Crows are circling in the sky, keepers of the local legend that birds of the same genus – corvus – guarded the Church of the Raven, which was dedicated to the Patron Saint Vincent, after he was buried on the Cape in the 300s. Meanwhile, back in the lantern-top on the Lighthouse, a Portuguese Captain of Lighthouses explains through an interpreter the tremendous candle power of the beacon's hyper radiant Fresnel*

> *lens. It is one of the largest ever built – in Paris
> – and able to flash once every two seconds since
> it came into service with a mechanical assembly
> in 1908.*

We continue. The road around Crows' Point passes through a sparse pine forest that parallels the long stretch of open, sandy beaches on the east coast, which the island's invaders have often crossed. Today, tourists are on these beaches. And some small villas and luxuriant grasses, ferns and flowering bushes in the area suggest a relatively moderate microclimate.

The road now runs straight along the east coast to Port Joinville. This town was still called Port Breton when the Revolution swept away religious privileges and it replaced Saint Sauveur as the capital in 1789. Port Breton was finally renamed Port Joinville in 1846 after a nephew of Louis XVIII had generously sponsored some modern public works. These included the construction in 1830 of the Grand Lighthouse at the northern end of the island, which served until the end of the German occupation in 1944, and major improvements to the harbour that included breakwaters. Around the port one would have seen the sailors with patched pants and blouses. And the tuna fishing fleets would have looked much the same until they disappeared by the 1950s: an organized chaos of masts, rigging, furled sails and hulls tilting in on each other.

III

Entering the walled compound of Île d'Yeu Communal Cemetery I find myself disoriented in a dense forest of grave crosses and crucifixes. In this part of the cemetery the tombstones seem to be aligned in rows, but they lie so close together that one's feet can get caught if one tries to cut too quickly across the rows to get around them. My throat tightens, causing me to choke momentarily in a physical reflex against the constricted space and the clutter of votive *bric-à-brac* and flowers, both artificial and real. These offerings do nothing to soften the unyielding, sharp-edged surfaces of masonry and stone.

Catching my breath, I follow Dominique to where his father's name takes shape on a headstone: Claude Turbé, 1932-1984. Set among other graves of similar design, Claude's tombstone is an elongated white one, carrying into eternity various votive tablets *à notre père, à notre grand-père, à notre beau-frère* and so on. Some glistening ceramic offerings of roses and pansies are on the same voyage. A white headstone cross supports the long metal crucifix that brands the grave.

The dates, which so starkly document Claude's life, make me think about its stages. He was a boy of eight to twelve years old when he lived through the German occupation and went to school hungry, while a German commandant ruled the island from the main hotel at Port Joinville. Was Claude a distracted pupil? Who can say today? The main fact for me is that he outlived the Nazi regime and made those pencil marks on the pages of my copy of Saint-Exupéry's book of resistance to it, *Pilote de guerre*. A central idea of the book, to which Claude's marks signed him up, is that just as each is responsible for all, France is responsible for the world. Had France stood in 1940, the world could have been galvanised into resistance by France. As Saint-Exupéry put it, *La France eût pu server au monde de clef de voutre,* France could have served as the keystone of the arch of the world.

The language was universal, ramblingly philosophical and oblique. If this means *Pilote de guerre* offers an elegiac account of war, this probably helped it in December 1942 to pass the German censor Gerhard Heller for publication with Gallimard in Paris. Despite a reference to *one of my friends <u>Léon Werth</u>*, the well-known Jewish writer (whose name Claude underlined), and despite many references to one Jean Israël, who Saint-Exupéry explains had a bright red nose and was the most heroic man in his squadron, Stacy Schiff in her, *Saint-Exupéry, a biography* (2009) says something that surprises me. Apparently, Heller only censored a single line in the book that no subsequent French edition has restored. This is the line, a considerable understatement many might think, referring to that *fool, Hitler, who unloosed this mad war.*

As I read that *keystone* passage, which Claude read before me, its implication is that resistance to barbarism was the only way for France to be herself and, by being herself, serve the world. Standing before Claude's humble tomb, my thoughts settle on the keystone of the arch of the world: civilisation – to which France has made its special contribution. Claude's reading of *Pilote de guerre* left many signs that he was a man who would have been likely to resist barbarism before he died at the age of fifty-two from what Dominique once told me was renal failure after eating shellfish. Faint pity comes over me at the arbitrary cause and timing of his death and, equally, of my own father's and mother's deaths. Faint happiness also that, as much as his death, Claude's life included a far-flung foreigner like me beneath the arch of the world.

Claude is not the only Turbé in the cemetery. The grave of his daughter Sophie – Dominique's younger sister – lies close to his. And now, as some space opens for me in the cemetery, a large polished black stone tomb, which indicates a family alliance, comes into view. Emblazoned in gold lettering the black stone reads: *Famille Turbé-Lecorf.*

One finds further references to the Turbé family on the World War One memorial that has a central location among the tombs and reaches higher than them all into the sky. On the stone cross at the top of the memorial The Saviour is represented by nothing more than his loincloth slung diagonally across its flat intersection, from top left to bottom right where it is secured with a knot. Vaporised. *REQUIESCANT IN PACE.*

Few towns in Australia with a population of 4,000 would have had the names of 130 men, over three percent of its people, inscribed on their *Great War* memorials. Other French towns would have more. But the point here is that Turbé is the name of nine of the 130 men from Île d'Yeu who are listed as having been killed during the war or died of wounds soon after it. Almost seven percent of the total. More strangely haunting, the names listed, which are arranged in chronological order by date of death, show that, while the first man from Île d'Yeu killed in the war in 1914 was M. Turbé, the last one killed in 1918 was E. Turbé.

Next stop: Marshal Pétain's tomb. Dominique turns one way, props, and moves in another direction. He has momentarily forgotten the way. And, as it happens, Pétain's tomb is out of alignment with all the others in the cemetery.

His tomb faces east; all the others face west, directly out to sea. Backed with pencil pines, his tomb is obscured on two sides by green shrubs. As I come through the scrub, stumbling into the open area at the foot of the grave, I am only partially aware of a wooden cross standing at the head of a

simple structure, solid, low, and white. With only
the words *Philippe Pétain Maréchal de France* inscribed on it, this is the grave of the man who was
deified after his victory at Verdun in 1916 made
him one of history's great defensive generals. Then,
the problem hits me: the grave has been desecrated, breaking up my view of it.

Cracks in history, fissures in the French past, into
which Pétain fell, once he became, as Saint-Exupéry put it in *Lettre A Un Otage* (1945), a *syndic
de faillite*, agent of bankruptcy.

At a time of cataclysmic collapse, Pétain rose
through vacant political ranks on the vanity of an
old soldier and of a false god. He felt indispensable. In late June 1940, he announced to the nation
that it was to receive *le don de ma personne* (the
gift of my person). At the age of 84, he became the
head of the government that was assembled from
failures and opportunists bobbing about in the
wake of defeat. This was at Vichy, the ornate spa
town specialising in bourgeois cures. There, subject
to the whims of the conqueror, Pétain became what
historian Robert Paxton's classic *Vichy France*
(2001) describes as a *blank image* of the country,

onto which people could project their desires for security and salvation from the abyss into which the country had fallen.

The reality was abysmal. The personality cult of the Marshal veiled an anti-Semitic collaborationist regime mouthing fascist slogans of *national revolution* and dependent on defeat for its existence. That regime may have created some semblance of order. It also deported Jews in larger than hitherto unfathomed numbers.

Vichy police fell in with the French gendarmerie in German occupied France. Together they were responsible for arresting over 80 percent of those detained in French holding centres until the Germans sent them on to their factories of death in the east. Vichy had special responsibility for arresting some 11,000 children. Eighty trains left France carrying human fuel for Auschwitz-Birkenau alone. Current research registers that a total of 75,721 people left France, of which only some 2,500 avoided the gas chambers. Furthermore, 60,000 political prisoners were deported from France for acts of resistance, while over 600,000 men were conscripted for forced labour in Germany – *le service de travail obliga-*

toire – of whom Monsieur Esseul mentions 60 were from Île d'Yeu. Vichy also squired murderous militias.

Perhaps it is easy for a foreigner to think like this. Things always look bad on the losing side. Yet Pétain's earlier greatness throws a strange light onto the bitter emptiness of his last command. Vichy was no keystone of the arch of the world; with that capital there was no arch. It is also unlikely that a foreigner was responsible for today's desecration. A thin marble slab resting against the foot of the grave and incised with the words *Our Uncle Philippe Pétain* has been cracked with a hammer. And close to this broken tablet, there are, disgustingly, recent turds at the tomb.

We move on quickly, with me thinking of a moment in Sydney not long after returning from one of my trips to Paris to research Vietnamese history. I remember being riveted by news of the former Vichy police chief René Bousquet. One day in June 1993, he answered the door of his Paris apartment and a furniture removalist shot him dead.

The others go on ahead of me in search of the

Australian graves, while I re-group in a shady area that the fall of the afternoon shadows locates beside the cemetery's western wall. Dark thoughts disappear as I look east and see a thousand crosses facing me, lit up gently in the afternoon sun.

The verticality of the view is dramatic. There is visionary lift-off within the compact space contained by the cemetery's walls, as the massed tombs seem to shake out into equidistant order and rise on the blue tide between earth and sky. Fresh white tombs, some with metal nameplates and icons glinting, are interspersed with old tombs that are blotched with lichen and pitted rusty brown or pumice grey. Standing together in a deep shadow three small, brooding stone crosses make a miniature Calvary. Some of the old tombs are propped up to prevent their sides falling away. Some family reliquaries stand in a row like a little street of houses. Some faces of the departed look back from the grave, fatally frozen in oval frames. With lit crosses for masts, this light stone fleet of graves is sailing westwards to where the sun sets on the ocean of eternity.

***

Île d'Yeu's past now brushes mine: the others have

found the Australians in the cemetery. Or almost, for the discovery reveals a case of confused identity. Daniel's meeting with us this morning had prompted him to remember Australian graves. But his memory was at variance with what we find: the resting place of four New Zealanders. What is more, the New Zealanders are buried with two Britons and a Canadian in a collective grave in a British Commonwealth War Grave Commission (CWGC) plot. This grave faces west, as do all the others, except Pétain's, and is in the last row beside the southern wall.

The words incised into the common headstone read: *These Seven Airmen Fell and were Buried Together.* The individual headstones, which are set like paving stones onto the surface of the tomb, detail a former Royal Air Force (RAF) composite Commonwealth Bomber Command crew.

> *R/77565 Warrant Officer II*
> *J.H. EKELUND*
> *Pilot*
> *Royal Canadian Air Force*
> *16 October 1942 Age 23*

> *NZ404353 Flying Officer*
> *M.S. GILBERD*
> *Observer*
> *Royal New Zealand Air Force*
> *16 October 1942 Age 28*

> NZ402823 Flight Sergeant
> E.H. HOWELL
> Wireless Operator/Air Gunner
> Royal New Zealand Air Force
> 16 October 1942 Age 21

> 1184443 Sergeant
> J.C. LEACH
> Wireless Operator/Air Gunner
> Royal Air Force
> 16 October 1942 Age 22

> NZ405737 Sergeant
> A. MARTIN
> Wireless Operator/Air Gunner
> Royal New Zealand Air Force
> 16 October 1942 Age 27

> NZ404970 Sergeant
> M.A. TORRANCE
> Air Gunner
> Royal New Zealand Air Force
> 16 October 1942 Age 30

> 522477 Sergeant
> E.H. UZZELL
> Flight Engineer
> Royal Air Force
> 16 October 1942 Age 25

Even though there were no Australians in this crew, its history is instantly intelligible to me: its formation was woven into the wider story of global expeditions from far-flung British settler societies arching fatefully back through space and time to what the Australian poet and correspondent of that war Kenneth Slessor called *the ancestral darkness of home.*

The New Zealanders were ANZACS, upholders of the joint Australian and New Zealand Army Corps tradition that was established in World War One and is influential in both countries to this day. The links to Canadian and British airmen had official foundations. Almost all airmen from the Dominions who fought over Europe began their odysseys with training in their home countries, with a large percentage undertaking further training in Canada under the Empire Air Training Scheme. There were smaller schemes in Africa for South Africans and Rhodesians. Advanced and operational training followed in England.

Operational casualties in Bomber Command were heavy. So also, a somewhat muted conversation with Dominique a few days ago in Nantes Cathedral forces me to recall, was the toll among civilians resulting from that Command's operations – in France as well as in Germany.

In the Cathedral we had ambled into the shadowy space of a memorial plaque to some 60,000 French civilians killed by Allied as well as German bombing after the D-Day landings in June 1944. These startling figures made me think immediately of 'Air War and Literature', by German writer W. G. Sebald. The essay was published in his collection of essays *On the Natural History of Destruction* and was still very much an eye opener when it came out in German in 1999 and English in 2003 – even as the most devastating air wars between 1945 and 2003 hardly close our eyes by comparison.[2]

Sebald's essay reaches for the limits of the atomic silence surrounding the *area-bombing* of German cities between 1942 and 1945, which killed over 600,000 civilians, while injuring many millions and destroying their homes. Significantly, the silence resounded in *especially post-war German literature.* Having attempted to sanitise the world of other peoples – having murdered and worked millions to death – Sebald thinks Germans were silenced by the rising fear that, as those surviv-

---

2. Recall the U.S. firebombing of Tokyo with napalm, which included, on the night of 9-10 March 1945 alone, the killing of as many as 100,000 people in the most destructive bombing raid in human history; the atomic bombings of Hiroshima and Nagasaki; and the U.S. bombing campaign against Vietnam, Cambodia, and Laos in 1964-73, which routinely employed napalm and was the most intense in human history.

ing in the rubble of their cities, they were the *rat people*. The swarming flies were another overpowering aspect of the death and destruction that had to be blocked out or generate more madness. Also, people can't grasp the prospect of boiling in their own fat; and it's hard to comprehend the appearance of crocodiles in the rubble of a European city, some writhing in agony, some crawling down the visitors' staircase after bombs hit the Berlin Zoo.

The essay's conclusion is overwhelming. It winds up from the hysterical German view that Jewish psychological specialists were behind the strategy for the destruction of German cities. It recalls the insane fantasy Hitler shared with his associates in 1940 about setting London on fire with the new incendiary bombs, a fantasy Goering would have realised if he could have. The bombing of Guernica, Warsaw, Belgrade, and Rotterdam was all the work of Germans. Then, after concluding that *we* [the Germans] *actually provoked the annihilation of the cities in which we once lived*, Sebald devotes the last sentence to how, in 1942, 1,200 German Nazi bombers hit Stalingrad killing 40,000 people when it was (like Dresden later) swollen with refugees.

I am unaware that firestorms were loosed on France. I am not sure either how much post-war French literature has to say about Allied bombing over France. There, in any case, such bombing was directed at German forces, not French civilians, so that the massacre of civilians and the smashing of their urban habitats was, as it is so clinically described today, *collateral damage* resulting from the imprecise nature of aerial bombardment on built up areas. (This includes twenty-first century missile and drone strikes on Middle Eastern wedding parties and bazaars, even though advanced technology makes bombing much more precise today). The 60,000 French casualties were quietly remembered in Nantes Cathedral. But my impression is that appalling number were also victims of the incapacity to process the shocking barbarism in which human beings routinely revel. *The need to know was at odds with a desire to close down the senses*, Sebald writes.

The Allied area bombing of German cities was undoubtedly one reason why Nazi leaders were not charged with mass bombing at the Nuremburg war crimes trials. Yet the aircrews were not responsible for Bomber Command's target selection. The Commander, Sir Arthur Harris, known as *Bomber Harris* in the press and as *Butcher Harris* in the RAF itself, was responsible for that.

Neither does target selection change the limited life expectancy of the members of those crews or what it took for them to confront it. Between 1940 and 1945, approximately 4,050 Australian airmen were killed in Bomber Command air operations, out of some 13,000 who flew over Europe. Total New Zealand operational deaths were 1,850 out of 6,000. (Precise records of neither the total number of Australians nor New Zealanders who flew were kept, as far as I know.) There were in the order of 60 white African, 10,000 Canadian and 40,000 British deaths.

What chain of events came down to the remains in the collective grave? Since the Battle of France in 1940, Bomber Command had been attempting to destroy railheads, docks, factories, and submarine pens in and around French cities; it had also been laying sea mines around ports. As I will learn later from various sources, most notably Errol Martyn's trilogy on New Zealand airmen *For Your Tomorrow* (1998-2008), the names listed on the collective grave were from 149 Squadron RAF based at Lakenheath in Suffolk. This was the squadron that was involved with two others in 3 Group Bomber Command in mine laying operations around the Biscay ports on the evening of 16th October 1942.

Thirty-four Wellington and Stirling bombers had taken off just after 1800 hours. Four did not return. One of these was hit by flak and crashed at Grandchamps-des-Fontaines, 17km from the centre of Nantes – remarkably close to where we are staying with the Dominiques at Le Temple de Bretagne. At least two of the other missing aircraft were also probably hit by flak around Nantes or St Nazaire (with its German submarine pens). One of those others crashed in the Bay of Biscay off Île de Ré not far from Île d'Yeu. The other was the Stirling from 149 Squadron captained by Canadian pilot John Herbert Ekelund, which took off at 1830 hours to lay mines in the Gironde estuary at Bordeaux and, within about two and a half hours, had crashed on Île d'Yeu.

In November 2012, in Sydney, seventy years and one month after that crash, I receive firsthand news of it. Errol Martyn, from Christchurch, will send me, from the New Zealand National Archives, a copy of the service record of Flying Officer Morris Searle Gilberd. A New Zealand Air Ministry letter in Gilberd's record is dated 11th February 1947 and addressed to his father in Wellington. This letter contains an English translation of a statement made by a Monsieur G. A. Champsaure in Paris:

> *During the first or second week in October 1942, shortly after 9 p.m., a bomber appeared over the island of Île d'Yeu coming from the direction of St. Nazaire. The motors were missing badly, and the plane seemed to be in great difficulty. Just before reaching the southern shore the plane burst into flames, and came down on the extreme south-western point of the little port of La Meule. The local inhabitants could not go out because of the curfew, and the Germans immediately rushed to the spot. They found debris scattered over a wide area, and the bodies of the aviators were buried in a communal grave the next day in the little cemetery at Port Joinville. It was thought that the aviators were trying to come down into the sea as the rafts were*

detached ready for release. The next day a fisherman near the spot found a Ronson cigarette lighter with the name Ekelund engraved on it.

Five years after the crash, the Gilberd family finally knew the circumstances of their irreparable loss. The Air Ministry letter implies that, since the Germans had only been able to identify two of the fallen airmen, namely Sergeants Torrance and Martin, it had, for some reason – perhaps missing paperwork – taken the discovery of Ekelund's lighter to enable the Ministry's identification of the entire crew. As a result, the letter continued, efforts were being made, in February 1947, to erect a cross over the grave bearing the names of all seven airmen. This was around the time that the CWGC would have established the collective grave in the form we now see it.

After receiving Champsaure's statement from Errol Martyn following our return from France, I will relay it to Dominique back in Le Temple de Bretagne. On a subsequent visit to the island in May 2013, he will find that, amazingly, Daniel's mother Madame Besseau saw the crash. As a child, she watched with her own eyes Ekelund's aircraft flying in flames in the night sky over her village at La Meule and crashing in a small inlet close to the port. She knew that the islanders were not permitted to go to the site until after the Germans had cleared it the next morning, and that people were saying the aircraft had been hit by German anti-aircraft fire over St Nazaire. Daniel's mother will further tell Dominique and Dominique that she had a ring fabricated out of debris from the plane's cabin.[3]

Meanwhile, in Sydney in November 2012, the internet will enable me to access the service record of Warrant Officer 2nd Class John Herbert Ekelund in the Canadian National Archives. *Jack,* to those close to him, came from Twin Butte, Alberta. The Canadian White Pages will provide two nearby telephone numbers for people named Ekelund. The second of these will be the right one. A member of the family will put me in touch with Jack's much younger cousin Muriel Eklund – different branches of the family have adopted different spellings of the family name. Conversations with excited,

---

3. I will not feel my link has broken with Daniel Besseau, who had told us he thought there were 'some Australians buried in the cemetery', or of course with his mother Madame Besseau, who saw on the evening of 16 October 1942 Jack's aircraft flying in flames over and crashing near La Meule, when news reaches me that Daniel passed away in mid-2022.

moved members of Jack's family in Alberta lie in the future: Jack's younger sister Helen was only three when he was killed; his younger brother Bob was thirteen.

They will talk to me for a long time. They will say that the family had received two letters from the Canadian War Ministry, one informing them that Jack was missing in action, the second some weeks later saying he was missing, presumed killed in action on a mission against the Biscay ports. Yet Bob and Helen will also say that they had never received confirmation of Jack's death and did not know its time and place. It seems, in fact, that I will give them the definitive information 70 years and two months after he fell.

It will be me who confirms that Jack was killed with the rest of his crew when their aircraft crashed at La Meule on Île d'Yeu; that his Ronson cigarette lighter had been found near the crash site; and that he was buried in a collective grave with his comrades in the Île d'Yeu Communal Cemetery.

They tell me that Jack came off a ranch, was very

bright at school, always wanted to be a pilot and went to the war to fight for his country. At the age of 73, Helen emphasises the heavy silence that settled around the subject of Jack's death in the family as she grew up – something that inhibited her from finding out about her big brother – plus the fact that their parents never recovered from the loss. Bob, who is 80, tells me that Jack had already flown his quota of operations, including some over Kiel and Cologne in Germany, but that his destiny had been to stand in for a friend on the night of 16th October 1942.[4]

Jack is the only member of the crew whose family I am able to contact; and the photo Bob has waiting to send me is special. This is the image of the whole crew, probably taken at Lakenheath, Suffolk. (See photo section). It was It was sometime after July 1942, when all four New Zealanders joined 149 Squadron, and before their last October evening. The airmen are lined up under the wing of their Stirling bomber from left to right: Gilberd,

---

[4.] Because of the immediate family connection Helen and Bob give me to Jack, I will not feel the link has broken with any of them when Muriel, with whom I will have had no contact since 2013, suddenly emails me from Canada on 31 May 2021 to ask me if I have yet published this book, and to inform me that, sadly, Bob and Helen had passed away in September and November 2019.

Howell, Torrance, Martin, Ekelund, Uzzell and Leach.

They are obviously dressed to kill. And, indeed, their combat clobber will loop back in my mind to Saint-Exupéry's account in *Pilote de guerre* of the warrior ritual of laborious dressing.

He recounts how he rigged himself out for his surveillance mission to Arras in three thick layers of clothing, heavy boots and in harnesses and assorted accessories that, like umbilical cords, brought the airmen into the being of the aircraft and vice-versa. He lists breathing masks, oxygen tubes, heating circuits and speaking tubes to support life and communications between the crew in their alien airborne environment – think especially of the air gunners in their exposed bubbles. Saint-Exupéry is ambivalent about this ritual. He indicates that, as they prepare for combat, deliberate heavy dressing functions to keep a warrior's attention on *immediate details*. Rather than think about saving the world from Nazism or, more vitally, about their own daunting prospects, they are preoccupied with the minutiae of slow dressing. He is most concerned about his gloves, where are his damned gloves? Yet he cannot entirely suppress the thought that this ceremony is readying him for the executioner.

Ekelund and his crew were no different. They were also experienced airmen. Ekelund and at least the three New Zealanders had flown well over 20 operations – Torrance 26. Like Saint-Exupéry, they knew the odds were stacked against them. Hence, the saddening, melancholy detail in the photo is, I think, the final immediate detail of their dressing for the camera: the near-smile or expression of fatalism in each case.

A probable flak attack around Nantes or Saint Nazaire would have legitimised their resignation. Saint-Exupéry has indicated how. He says that when his aircraft came under heavy anti-aircraft fire on the way to Arras, the world split open around him. After an initial spasm of terror, he feels he is floating at the centre of all things; his life comes before him; all his memories, needs and, not least, *mon enfance qui se perd comme une racine dans la nuit*, my childhood, which loses itself like a root in the night. This detached floating sensation is close to what I felt when, as I have described elsewhere, I had an out of body experience after being blown up by a mine in Vietnam. As Saint-Exupéry puts it, the combat stops his life and restarts it *sur la mélancolie d'un souvenir*, on the melancholy of a memory.

He was fatalistic to the last. And, aside from the war pilot's own texts, Stacy Schiff's biography and François Gerber, *Saint-Exupéry, écrivain en guerre* (2012) are works that illuminate for me his own narrative of wartime dejection: *j'ai l'impression de marcher vers les temps les plus noirs du monde; ça m'est bien égal d'être tué en guerre*, I feel that I am approaching the blackest time of the world; it is all the same to me, if I am killed at war.

After the fall of France, Saint-Exupéry went to America, where he became depressed and drank heavily. He had not only lost his country, but in three weeks his II/33 Squadron had lost seventeen crews out of 23. His literary fortunes contributed

The Beacon Tower

The Foghorn Station

The Cabins

Dominique's Flowers

Old Château

La Chapelle

La Route des Corbeaux

The Grave of Claude Turbé (1932-1984) in the Île d'Yeu Communal Cemetery

Île d'Yeu Communal Cemetery, in which all the headstones face west, except Pétain's, which faces east.

The Collective British Commonwealth War Grave of Jack Ekelund and his men in the Île d'Yeu Communal Cemetery.

Jack Ekelund and his whole crew under the wing of their Stirling Bomber sometime before it crashed on Île d'Yeu on 16 October 1942. Left to right: Gilberd, Howell, Torrance, Martin, Ekelund, Uzzell, and Leach. (Courtesy Bob Ekelund.)

The entrance to the Fort

Old aerial view of Fort de Pierre Levée. (Collection Maurice Esseul)

Inside Fort de Pierre Levée

Port Joinville, 15 July 2012

to his problems: *Pilote de guerre* issued in French by Gallimard in Paris in December 1942 did not receive the enthusiastic reception of the New York English language edition, published earlier the same year as *Flight to Arras.*

Pilote de guerre seems to have had a devoted clandestine readership. But soon, the Free French were officially frowning on the book, because of its publication in occupied France. At the same time, vicious, anti-Semitic, collaborationist critics and the German authorities there were catching up with the references to red-nosed Jean Israël and examining those parts about <u>the victory to come</u>. The German censor Gerhard Heller was severely reprimanded by his superiors and briefly placed under house arrest for permitting the book's publication in 1942. Gallimard did not reprint it in 1944.

Saint-Exupéry, who was still in America, still drinking heavily, wrote *Le Petit Prince*, which is one of the greatest children's stories in world literature, before rejoining II/33 Squadron, which had reformed in Algeria. Redeploying to Bastia in Corsica, he is remembered for expressing indifference to life and writing gallantly to his wife Consuelo saying the only regret he would have if he were shot down was that it would make her cry. Overweight and, at 44, too old to be flying, he took off from Bastia around 0830 on 31st July 1944 for a mapping mission around his birthplace in Lyon – he was born there on the morning of 29th June 1900 at 8 rue de Peyrat – and was never seen again.

***

We have no history without continuity or without change going on continuously around it. The shared fatalism of Saint-Exupéry and of Ekelund and his men and the fact that they fell in the same war for civilization are reasons why I feel the intersection of their destinies, right here at their Collective Grave in Île d'Yeu Cemetery. Claude and Sophie Turbé are also in the cemetery and my reading of Claude's reading of *Pilot de guerre* further evokes these correspondences now and in the future.

My discovery later in the year of the fisherman's find of Ekelund's Ronson lighter at La Meule 70 years before will make me think back to another fisherman's find. This was, indeed, the news, from 1998, that a fisherman trawling off the coast of Marseilles had plucked out of his net a silver identity bracelet with the words Antoine and Saint-Exupéry inscribed on it. Some cleaning of the bracelet further revealed the address of his New York literary associates Reynal and Hitchcock and the name of his wife Consuelo. Fifty-four years after Saint-Exupéry disappeared, the world finally knew he had fallen – for still unknown reasons – into the sea. *The ocean is so wide and a bracelet so small,* the fisherman is reputed to have exclaimed. *It is a miracle.*

Death changes the world. It is forever precipitating new arrangements and relations among the living. Fishermen will go on catching old-new facets of the dead in these shoals of time. But death is final. It is irredeemable loss. There will always be something about the past that is impossible to know.

The circumstances of the crash that killed Jack and his crew are in that realm. It is likely that the aircraft was out of control before it hit the ground, because no calculated crash-landing would have been attempted in the small surface area available on the flat southwest headland of La Meule. We know little more about what happened than that.

Champsaure's statement about the *rafts* being *detached ready for release* suggests an attempted crash-landing on water at night. This statement could be cross-examined. According to Errol Martyn, individual dinghy kits were stacked in racks inside the Stirling and these may have been detached. But that was not true of the Type J Dinghy for eight men. This piece of equipment was stowed in the Port wing and could not be released before hitting the sea. It was, moreover, the only dinghy that fits a raft description. Other issues could be raised, including questions of Champsaure's grasp of the terminology and, perhaps, of translation.

It still seems most unlikely that, if the aircraft flew over the island from the direction of St Nazaire and reached La Meule on the west coast, and if the pilot was still conscious, he was attempting to crash-land on the island. Bob will tell me that, once before, on finding himself in a tight spot during a training flight in Canada, Jack had crash-landed on water. He might have been trying to do that again. Assuming that the badly missing engines had been hit by flak, the fuel tanks or lines may also have been hit. This could have caused such flames as Champsaure said were seen and Madame Besseau saw. Furthermore, any detonation of the unexpended mines could have had a major bearing on the aircraft's final moments. Whatever happened, my impression is that Jack attempted to ditch into the sea but didn't make it. A point came where everything went black and spinning out of control the aircraft hit the land.

For the most part we can only imagine. Looking into the blue sky, which is made softer by light accumulations of fine cloud, I try to fix an arc in the firmament above Île d'Yeu Communal Cemetery and imagine what was going on inside that aircraft as it came into crash in what was a ball of flame some years before I was born.

IV

One more puzzle sealed in that time; one more stop. About a kilometre due west from the cemetery, through a forest, but a few kilometres away by road is Fort de Pierre Levée. It is where former Marshal Pétain was detained during the last six years of his life.

We remain silent as the jeep skirts around the spiky tree line; the subject, still unsettled in French history, is the Marshal's descent into exile. The defilement of his dignified, though deliberately misaligned tomb, which was waiting for us today, bears out that unease – as certainly as it flattened momentarily my low voltage, lingering interest in his fate. In fact, the levelling emptiness of that moment makes me wonder what his troubled legacy in recent French history might mean for an Australian at all.

My thoughts turn in the forest to the shadow I've always felt World War Two threw over my Australia, not from the nearby Pacific but from faraway Britain. It wasn't that, as I grew up in post-war Australia, the tropical horrors of the Pacific war with Japan weren't registered. They were, sometimes together with intense animosity towards the Japanese. At the same time, however, the general course of our British cultural recognition deflected us from taking a detailed interest in what happened in our near north. Just as, by extension, the weight of British or, in my present situation, French cultural recognition overwhelms one as an Australian who stays for any time in Britain or France or, for that matter, other western European countries. There, it seems, the density of what is culturally familiar can weigh so heavily on one's sense of the hemispheric distance from Australia, that an independent sense of Australian identity can go missing. For most of us, after all, that is a part of what it means to be Australian.

For me, the silence in the jeep is loaded with a sense of the embattled moral centre of my boyhood reading: the heart of the empire, Britain, of course. Clammy accounts came inevitably like ash in the air from the crematoria in Europe. But their ghastliness was so great they were difficult to take in; so difficult one suspects we had to normalise them. Flying higher than that unsettling sickness, in any case, *The Great Escape* (1950), *The Dambusters* (1951), and *Reach for the Sky* (1954), the biography of British air ace Douglas Bader, all by Australian RAF fighter pilot and German prisoner of war Paul Brickhill, were the kind of stories that got to me. *Biggles*, set in more exotic imperial outposts was in the mix. What teenage boy doesn't want to be a part of a war story on the other side of the world, anyway?

A few stories – *I Flew for the Fuhrer: The Story of a German Airman* (1953) by Heinz Knoke and *Samurai* (1957) by legendary Japanese air ace Saburo Saki – came from the other side.

Then, eventually in 1990, when the Bloomsbury paperback edition of the *New Yorker Book of War Pieces: London 1939 - Hiroshima 1945*, came out, the iconic photograph on its cover evoked my instant recognition. I felt part of the event it depicted, even though it pre-dated me by several years.

Either side of my birth in 1947, Singapore had fallen in 1942, Saigon in 1975. Any illusion of the permanence of western, including British imperial power in our part of the world should have been shattered. Yet, there it still was – in 1990. Instant recognition of the unshaken image on the cover of that book still seemed to fix the moment before my time that had forever cast its shadow over my life: London, probably late 1940, during the blitz, the dome of St Paul's Cathedral stands unmoved in the deep rumbling in the earth, as grainy puffs of grey smoke rise and an airy rain of dark particles fall around it.

From around the same time, when Germany seemed an unknowable heart of darkness, Pétain's empty image floated in puffy clouds over the kingdom of compromise and nothingness that, in my understanding of World War Two, became the anti-body of the empire.

By late 1940, Paris was, as one of the *New Yorker* stories described it, *in limbo*. There, Parisians were saying the German occupiers were *corrects*, meaning that, as if the aura of the city had put the barbarians on their best behaviour, they moved around it with disciplined, military-social decorum; and, also, *emmerdeurs,* a term that would never have been used in polite society before the occupation, meaning boring pests, who were, with excremental implications, bogging the place down. Soon, with the sinister fleet of black Citroëns parked outside Gestapo headquarters on Avenue Foch – into which address the Indochina Section of the French Foreign Intelligence Service moved in 1945 – that nuisance deepened and broadened into something more archetypical than Parisian conceit: the elemental human struggle between good and evil. It's rightly said that the Nazi occupation of France set up the great morality play of the twentieth century.

The play's resonance was clear in my reading of, for instance, *Reach for the Sky*. Therein, Bader loses his legs in a plane crash and heroically returns later to flying as a fighter pilot. After that, I've always remembered the bit about how, when the Germans captured him, he threw his legs at them. So it was that, much later, shocked by news that a Duntroon Military College classmate of mine had his legs blown off in a shell explosion in Vietnam, an absurd thought came to me; *he must have read Brickhill's Bade*r. And, as an Australian hero he probably had, (although one doesn't have to read a book to be influenced by it). And those thoughts were later confirmed in my mind when my friend joined a parachuting club, and the story went around that one of his legs fell off during a jump. There were many other incidents in books and films that I've forgotten, which inclined me, in the 1970s, into a fascination with the French Resistance.

Was there not a glistening black Nazi German backdrop, against which the Resistance rose with shining virtue and steadfast, finally irresistible British-American support to re-take the soul of France?

Notionally, one thinks. But that was far from all. In 1975, two months before the fall of Saigon, my resignation from the Army came through, and, in an undergraduate European history seminar at the University of Sydney, Paxton's earlier mentioned *Vichy France* came to my attention. Premised by that regime's dependence on both failure and an absence of resistance, the doubly unsettling thing

about Pétain for me was that, stepped back from
the nightmares of SS insignia and Gestapo torture
chambers in occupied France, though still in their
thrall, his Vichy regime was the last limbo. It was a
place of submission to German-cum-French fascist
terror, the dull hell that, during the war, was closer
to historical reality for most French people than
resistance.

France accommodated in considerable measure
the evil that Germany propagated. After the Allied
landing in France in 1944, Pétain's doctor, the
gifted French fascist writer Louis-Ferdinand Céline
knew this. He, along with his wife, cat, and an actor-friend, had followed his patient, Pétain, when
he fled to Germany at the head of a train of 1,400
Vichy officials, wives, mistresses, flunkies, and
Nazi *protectors*. This group occupied the medieval
castle at Siegmaringen on the Danube, where it
became the centerpiece of Céline's blackest novel
D'un château l'autre (1957).

In this barely fictional masterpiece, written in startlingly fractured idiomatic language, the group's
existence in the castle is dominated by terror at
the constant threat of air raids. Sirens are forever

wailing. Orgies erupt and toilets explode as the castle's bad plumbing succumbs to the pressure of overuse. Starvation was an interminable preoccupation; food coupons and bread rolls are assiduously eyed-off and counted.

Towards the middle of the story, Pétain, and here I quote from Ralf Manheim's translation of Céline's novel, *the last king of France*, leaves the drawbridge of the castle and leads a procession of his generals and admirals and hangers-on along the banks of the Danube. Bombs are falling; *how did they manage to miss! ... their bombs sent up gysers! The Danube is boiling!* The RAF is machine gunning the area and attacking a bridge, which it never seems to hit either. General Bridou, the thinly disguised Bridoux, who had been a Minister for War in the Vichy government, *finished pissing in the bushes ... he shook it ... thoroughly! and then he said: Gentlemen we must Act. He came out with his idea ... We must scatter ... the cavalry principle....*

Is Pétain gaga? Can he not hear the bombs and the sirens? According to Céline, who names himself as the narrator in the novel, *you can take it from me that if he* [Pétain] *hadn't taken command there at the bridge, if he hadn't got that procession started, there would never have been any High Court ... or Nouguarès either.* This is a fiercely ironic reference to the High Court of Justice that tried high-profile collaborators after the Liberation and its president Louis Nouguarès. Céline goes on with a reference that implies the hypocrisy of Nouguarès and the courage of Pétain, who decided to return to France in April 1945 to face his accusers: *if not for him and his cool head ...no one would have got out from under that arch* [of the bridge] *it would have been all over! no indictment! no verdict! no hash! no need for the Île d'Yeu either!*

This is the only reference to the island in Céline's novel – and there may not be many more in all French *belles-lettres* either. As the remote place to where the former President of Vichy was eventually banished, however, that single backhand reference to Île d'Yeu signifies the speck in the ocean of ambiguity that played a significant role in pulling the uncertain French state together and anchoring it post-war.

A common theme in the murky political crosscurrents between fascist and free France can be discerned. In Céline's novel, *Charlot*, the Charlie Chaplin figure *you never saw in the trenches with a bazooka* is a parody of de Gaulle. Yet de Gaulle was also to write, as Céline had, of Pétain's *courage* in returning to France to face his accusers.

Other ambiguities abound. History records that, in August 1945, the High Court of doubtful impartiality convicted Pétain of treason for concluding an armistice with the Germans but showed little interest in such matters as Vichy's deportation of Jews and political prisoners and sending of forced labour to Germany. After sentencing Pétain to death, the court recommended life imprisonment, because of his advanced age – and, no doubt, because of his troubling former greatness.

De Gaulle, then a great figure and head of the Provisional Government, had good reasons to ratify the court's recommendation. He had been a protégé of Pétain's in the inter-war period. He had also been an outlaw. As leader of the Free French resistance, de Gaulle had been condemned in absentia by the Vichy government for treason and desertion, and so, now, with their positions reversed, he could not have been indifferent to the fate of his old superior. As the court passed sentence on Pétain and stripped him of his Marshal's Képi, de Gaulle made his own aircraft available to fly the prisoner into the south of France where he was detained in the bleak prison fortress at Le Portalet, high in the Pyrénées near the Spanish border.

Still, in the aftermath of the German occupation, an insecure government feared Pétain's presence on the mainland might help to focus opposition forces and cause a civil war. For that reason, the government moved him in mid-November to Île d'Yeu.

The Charles Williams biography *Pétain* (2005) tells us about the move. In the dead of night, 15 November, an armed convoy of five cars with him in the third one left Le Portalet. One of the cars broke down at Bordeaux the next morning and the locals gawked at Pétain while it was being fixed in a garage. Still fearing ambushes, the party avoided the usual port of departure for the island at Fromentine and, late in the morning, reached the Atlantic coast at the fishing village of La Pallice.

There, the prisoner was placed on board a French navy corvette, which departed for the island at noon the next day, 16 November. During the voyage he held court in the captain's rooms, reminiscing about the warm welcome he had received from the fishing community on Île d'Yeu when he had visited in 1921. The crossing ended in bad weather. The corvette was unable to dock at Port Joinville and Pétain's inauspicious landing occurred after he was transferred to a fishing boat towed by a launch. Stepping ashore at his place of exile, he turned to an impassive crowd and raised his Homburg.

In the meantime, France's former colony in Indochina had been lost to the Japanese. When the Japanese were in turn defeated in August 1945, Ho Chi Minh's Democratic Republic of Vietnam (DRV) seized power, and he declared its independence on 2nd September.

To re-take Indochina de Gaulle's Provisional Government raised a French Expeditionary Force. To do so rapidly, and straight after the European war, that government recruited former SS soldiers, many no doubt on the run from the law. The force that attacked the DRV's Government's offices in Saigon on 27 September 1945 and initiated Vietnam's thirty-year war of national independence had marched straight out of the ambiguities of recent French history. During that war, orders in some French Foreign Legion units had to be given in German.

V

Our jeep stops abruptly in the forest at the grim portal of Fort de Pierre Levée. A wooden bridge crosses a moat and reaches a passage leading further into a courtyard through an arched entrance in a wall. The dates 1858-1866 appear above the arch.

Even in summer, the dreariness of the vista is intensified by the flat expanse of the wall, which extends about 60 metres either side of the entrance and rises about 12 metres from the bottom of the dry moat, about 20 metres wide. One looks down into an unsettling wilderness of yellow and green grasses. Dark green foliage spills over the outer wall of the moat, as the forest pushes up all around. Dominique leans forward in the driver's seat and points up to an odd-looking structure sitting on top of the wall above the arch. *Pétain a habité là,* he says. Pétain lived there.

It is not easy to imagine Pétain doing that. Entering the square courtyard-cum-parade ground, the harsh glare rebounding off its surface makes it difficult to focus on any surrounding point. Looking blankly in on the square, I find the uniformity of the fort's opaque inner walls rising five or six metres above the yard further repels scrutiny. Again, denying a point of reference, the walls heighten the effect of feeling enclosed in this large, isolating, perhaps 85 metres square space. Today, it is difficult to reconcile this feeling with the social uses to which the Fort has been and will be variously put: a holiday colony since the 1960s, a second municipal hall beneath a marquee in the square, a place where community fêtes and weddings take place. The old barracks will also house various club rooms – music, photography, hunting, fishing – and a museum.

It is a relief to open Monsieur Esseul's *Petite histoire*. It says that Fort de Pierre Levée was built on Île d'Yeu as part of a wider scheme Napoleon III had undertaken to enhance France's coastal defences and that military engineers had sited it on the island's highpoint, the hill known as Pierre Levée. Yet here in the citadel there is no sense of it standing on a hill. And it takes some looking at the aerial photo in the text to work out why not. The answer lies in the wide area of grassed earth sandwiched between the outer curtain wall and inner wall or redoubt of the fortress, as one sees them from a bird's eye view. (Although in the image in the photo section, the building on stilts at the rear of the parade ground, the trees lining the square on three sides, and the two grassed mounds sloping down from the bulwark with foot tracks on them at the rear of the fort do not exist today.)

Rather than show that the citadel was built on top of the hill, the photo shows that it has been built *in place* of the hill. Relating the photo to what is around me, I realise that to develop the fortifications the top of the hill *was sliced off*, leaving the feature truncated. A depression dug out in an excavated plane created the parade ground, leaving earthen walls, with their formats squared within the irregular shape of the original hill, to be reinforced on both sides around it. The building of the outer curtain walls and inner redoubt either side of the earth walls then provided an approximately

17-metre-wide bulwark for the parade ground. Casements used as barracks or cells, stables and storerooms were dug into the earth between the walls.

Designed to hold the men who would defend these walls and sally forth from them if the island's gun batteries were overrun, the fort has replaced with formidable snugness a former hill in the middle of the forest. Altogether, the outer walls are about 120 metres square – with arrowhead bastions at each corner – and the moat about 20 metres wide. The citadel is thus about 160 metres square.

Pétain's residence, which seems to have been converted from a former guardhouse, is perched over the portal of all this. Between 1874 and 1912, *Petite histoire* notes that companies of the 93rd Infantry Regiment from La Roche-sur-Yon were rotated through the garrison. Yet these men were not tested by an invasion, and, in any case, the island's relative remoteness meant that the fortress' first function had become that of a political prison.

***

Pétain's predecessors had been brought to the

island since 1871, when insurgents taken during the suppression of the Paris Commune were briefly held here. They were soon sent on to exile in Noumea, one of the far-flung destinations in the global history of the French prison island empire. Devils' Island off the coast of French Guiana was where another alleged traitor, Alfred Dreyfus, was held; and where the bodies of dead prisoners were fed to sharks. Another was Puolo Condor off the southern coast of Vietnam where thousands of members of the Indochinese Communist Party were held in brutish conditions during the inter-war years.

Conditions for the detainees from the Central Powers held on Île d'Yeu during World War One remained deplorable. The detainees included Germans, Austrians, Hungarians, Bulgarians, Gypsies, Czechs, and Turks from all walks of life. And a unique view of the suffering of those people is presented in a major work of Hungarian literature by Transylvanian writer Aladár Kuncz, whose book *Fekete kolostor* (Budapest, 1931) appeared in Ralph Murray's persuasive English translation under the title *Black Monastery* (London, 1934). Later French translations of the Hungarian rendered the title as *Le Monastère noir* (1937, 1999, 2014).[5]

Kuncz had been a translator of French literature, whose sojourn in France on a scholarship from his government in 1913 turned into a five-year-long-nightmare. He was detained in August 1914 and held from October that year in the medieval château-monastery at Noirmoutier-en-île, an island just off Fromentine. Looking south from the dark tower there, he tells us that he had line of sight

---

[5.] See the French *Wikipédia* entry for Aladár Kuncz. With the agitations of literary critics, most notably Régis Messac, who read Murray's 1934 English translation, and who wrote of the *power* and *universal significance* of the book's *terrible pages*, Gallimard published a French language translation and adaptation, *Le Monastère noir*, in Paris in 1937. German, Italian, and Turkish editions followed. Not far from both Île de Noirmoutier and Île d'Yeu in the Vendée at Beauvois-sur-mer, L'Étrave recently published new editions of *Le Monastère noir* in 1999 and 2014. Writing in 2007, another French author Jean-Léon Muller emphasises the *longevity* of French interest in Kuncz's work. He references several French studies of World War One, immigration, and prison or detention regimes, which note *Le Monastère noir*, including Jean-Claude Farcy, *Les camps de concentration de la Première Guerre mondiale (1914-1920)*, Paris, Economica, 1995.

In Australia, the dissemination of Kuncz's work is another story. After being alerted in 2021 to its existence by Dominique, I initially assumed it only had a French translation, *Le Monastère noir*, which I tried but failed to obtain. Dominique couldn't find copies in the Vendée either. But then, on stumbling over the existence of Murray's 1934 English translation while reading Kuncz's *Wikipédia* entry, I was pleasantly surprised to find that there was a copy of that English version in the National Library of Australia (NLA). I had in fact found that the 1934 London publication of Murray's translation by Chatto and Windus had been received in real time in 1934 in Canberra by the NLA's precursor, the Commonwealth Parliament Library, (which had been created in 1901 and continued to be the Parliamentary Library after 1960, when the NLA was created as a separate entity). On learning that no request had been made for the NLA's copy of the book since digital records began in 2008, I indulged a hunch while reading it. My intuition was that 87 years after a copy of the English version of Kuncz's work reached Australia, I was the first one to read it. The feeling that no other reader had opened the pages of the book and cast their eyes over them before me, gave me a special sense of communion with the past and, it seemed, of closeness to Kuncz's 90-year-old original – even though he wrote it in Hungarian.

across the water to Île d'Yeu.

Stories circulating among the detainees in Noirmoutier further indicated that the citadels there and on Île d'Yeu were a part of a wider network of grim detention facilities in other parts of the country, including the Vendée at Sables D'Olonne, Luçon, and Fontenay-le-Comte. It was said of those places that *typhoid broke out in one of the family camps ... more than half the children died...* There was talk of *the death camp at Sables D'Olonne.*

In August 1916, when Kuncz was moved from the Noirmoutier *madhouse* and into the *catacombs* of Fort de Pierre Levée on Île d'Yeu, he says *that the lid closed on the coffin of my life. Owls like black rags thrown in the air rose from the moat and hooted in an uncanny rhythm over the citadel at night.* Perhaps 200 men were crammed into the airless underground casements with an area of *80 cms x 1.8 m long* for their straw palliasses. By the winter of 1917, severely malnourished, weakened, and mentally unbalanced by their captivity, the miserable prisoners were plagued by ... *the foul, bloody waters of the War which kept them imprisoned.*

Still far from release, however, the Armistice of November 1918 would mark the intensification of their suffering. The end of the war and continuation of their captivity for many months coincided on Île d'Yeu with the arrival of the Spanish Flu. Without care, medicines, or hygiene, the detainees were left moaning and vomiting in the casements.

Between Christmas and New Year 1919, when *the illness came with a rush, seizing every man in the citadel*, perhaps half of them died. Kuncz's own destiny was to be released in May and return to Budapest, where he took twelve years to die, aged 46, in June 1931, a few weeks after the publication of his book.

Then, many years later, in the afterlife of its author, I will find myself surprised by an antipodean association that parallels the former French world prison island archipelago and globalises his story of World War One internment on Île d'Yeu. The association will also result in a doubling of my visit to the island.

In 2018, I will meet Gerhard Fischer, a professor of German literature in Sydney. Gerhard is also the author of *Enemy Aliens: internment and the home-front experience in Australia, 1914-1920 (1989)*, which is the definitive history of the irreparable damage done to the German Australian community in World War One. It shows how the old eighteenth-nineteenth century British-Australian prison island ethos, which had shadowed – with the gallows rather than the guillotine – the old French one, made something of a come-back in 1914-1920.

In those years, the main Australian *Concentration Camp* for German Australians was at Holsworthy near Liverpool in Sydney. Chapter 10 of *Enemy Aliens* covers the offshore islands that set up the association with Noirmoutier-en-île and Île d'Yeu around the same time: Bruny, just south of Hobart; Rottnest, off Perth; and Torrens Island in the bleak tidal swamp of Port Adelaide estuary. New Zealand also detained people of German derivation on various prison islands, including on Soames Island in Wellington Harbour, while still others were held by the British on Stonecutters Island in Victoria Harbour, Hong Kong.

Of the Australian Islands, Torrens was said to be the *worst*. Detainees were *whipped*, *chained to trees*, and pricked during bouts of *indiscriminate bayoneting*. *Promiscuous shooting* by guards occurred, although it does not seem to have killed or seriously injured anyone. The milder Australian winters break down to some extent the parallel with Île d'Yeu. So does the relatively slight effect of the Spanish Flu in Australia. Perhaps a few score in over six thousand detainees were afflicted in the main Camp at Holsworthy.

But still, Gerhard's story echoes Kuncz's story in mine; so much so that, indeed, something wholly inconceivable to me at the Fort in 2012 will happen following my narrative of my visit to it. The fact is that on a trip to Europe in 2019 Gerhard will be staying in the Vendée, and having read an early draft of my story, he will make a side-visit to Île d'Yeu.

Soon after his visit to the island he will dispatch by email his *Salut de La Vendée*:

> *I'm spending a few days with my friends in Sables d'Olonne, and we visited Île d'Yeu today in your footsteps! Unfortunately, very cold, rainy, and*

> *stormy; it's* hors de saison *with lots of places closed, and we didn't have enough time to drive around, but we did manage the cemetery and citadel and walk around the harbour. I started reading your story again to connect the dots between life and literature ...*

One thing with the space and time to link those disparate things is history. I did not mention earlier that, in 1564, long before Gerhard stayed at Sables d'Olonne, Protestants from La Chaume, a suburb of that city, and from La Rochelle launched a punitive campaign against Catholics and their establishments along the coast of the Vendée and on Île d'Yeu. While people crowded into the Old Château for protection, the invaders desecrated the statuary in Saint Sauveur Church and burnt Saint Étienne monastery before they departed. Four hundred and fifty-five years later, Gerhard will come via my narrative and others to visit memorials of still further wars. One site of memory he visited was *the cemetery*. Although a place of imprisonment rather than of protection since 1871, the other site of memory that we've seen he visited was the *citadel*, the Old Château's successor, Fort de Pierre Levée.

Early in World War Two, the Fort was still a facility for the disposal of political castaways. During the so-called phony war in 1940, Monsieur Esseul records that the postal boat *Insula-Oya* docked at Port Joinville on 10 May carrying 282 communist deputies and mayors, whom the government had found undesirable and so consigned to the Fort. Perhaps, like Kuncz and his group, they were repelled by their quarters. But this time their tenure in the underground casements was short. Presumably, because the Germans needed them as barracks for their own garrison and did not want to feed prisoners, they returned them to prisons on the mainland after they occupied the island in June.

With the defeat of the Germans and the uncertainties of the French government in Paris, Île d'Yeu was readied for its most famous political prisoner.

***

Pétain's time in the Fort had come. Looking up at the windows from which he looked down into the courtyard over 70 years ago, my eyes find a place to rest in the shadow slanting over them. At the same time, I am thinking of the last chapter in Charles Williams' biography, *Pétain* (2005), which quotes an observation by one of the old Marshal's lawyers, who visited him about late 1947. The lawyer said he had slipped into an *eternal night*.

Former member of the Resistance, Doctor Albert Massonie, who was entrusted with Pétain's care in 1949, kept a clinical journal of his decline *J'ai soigné Pétain*, which was finally published in 2017. What follows, however, is my non-specialised paraphrase of the last chapter of the Williams biography.

By 1948, the props supporting Pétain could not stave off his depression, talking about Vichy, Napoleon, and Verdun – you cannot imagine the complexity of large battles – and confusing these subjects and babbling in his sleep. Pétain's rooms were sparsely furnished with a metal bed, a chest of drawers, two chairs, a table, and an armchair. He had a stove in each room and a small adjacent bathroom and lavatory. Guards carried water in buckets from a distant tap. He ate alone. He took exercise in this square. Apart from the prison governor and five guards, those closest to him included his first Île d'Yeu physician Doctor Immanuel Imbert. Imbert drank too much, chased sailors, and led a group of them to break up the hotel at Port Joinville. In a histrionic outburst, he accused the owner of profiting from his denunciations of people to the Gestapo during the Occupation. The authorities wondered if he was a suitable person to tend such a distinguished prisoner.

It seems that Imbert cared well for Pétain and proved to be good company. Abbé Germain Pontheau, who had been among Pétain's many clerical sympathisers in the Vendée, was his confidant and took his confession once a week. Pétain's wife Nini also visited. As a discreet *roué*, his relationship with her had long been difficult. But she still basked in the prestige of being a Marshal's wife, and his dependence on her became childlike. In 1950, as his physical health fluctuated, the cover of *Paris Match* published a report from *Nos Reporters à L'Île d'Yeu: Le Maréchal avait préparé le gâteau du 95è anniversaire*, Our Reporters on Île d'Yeu: The Marshal has made his 95th birthday cake. The cover photo featured Nini, the cake and 95 candles – red, white, and blue.

In mid-1951, after great deliberation, President Vincent Auriol, an old socialist and one of the 80 Deputies who had voted against the extraordinary powers given to Pétain on 10 July 1940, designated the house of lawyer Paul Luco at 27 rue Gabriel Guist'hau, Port Joinville an annex of the Military Hospital in Nantes. This was so that Pétain could be moved there to die in a more congenial setting. This he did, as Williams puts it, *a troubled old man*, on the morning of 23 July 1951, with his great niece, her son, and his lawyers in attendance, and with a nurse holding his hand and a nun saying a rosary in the corner. Nini kissed his forehead.

VI

With Pétain's death, the tug of war over his grave began. My understanding is that he had wanted to be buried at Douaumont in the northeast of the country alongside those who fell at Verdun. But the state interred him on Île d'Yeu, thus extending the condition of exile to his remains.

Verdun veterans, who had demonstrated in French cities on the anniversary of the victory of battle each year of his living exile, flooded the island for his funeral; accompanied by bishops and generals. Beginning in 1968, every President since de Gaulle has, on the anniversary of the Verdun victory, sent flowers to his grave, while steadfastly excluding his leadership of the Vichy government from official notice. Such official ambiguity may have been necessary, of course, to suppress the darkly troubling wartime inheritance. As one might expect, the desecration of Pétain's tomb we stumbled over was far from the first. Dominique mentions other cases, reaching back to the 1950s. Most sensational, however, were the events of February 1973 when grave robbers lifted Pétain's coffin from his tomb and took it away.

Dominique will send to me in Sydney, from the Vendée newspaper *Ouest France* for 20-23 February 1973, full coverage of that amazing story. Madame Besseau had kept the clippings on Île d'Yeu at the time, and he obtained them from her during his May 2013 visit there.

Stupefaction on Île d'Yeu as in all France, declared *Ouest France* on Tuesday 20 February 1973. At 8.45 am the previous day, gravedigger Jean Taraud noticed the conspicuous cleanliness of the borders around Pétain's tombstone. On close inspection he was staggered to find that, despite careful attempts to camouflage what had happened, the 650 kg stone had been removed and replaced – with fresh cement – a centimeter out of alignment. At 3.30 pm a phalanx of officials both insular and continental met at the grave. The order was given to retract the tombstone half-way. An employee from the funeral company dropped into the hole and found that, indeed, the coffin containing the Marshal's remains had disappeared.

An investigation was opened. The wild barking of dogs in the area between 2 and 2.30 am, Monday 19 February suggested the time of the heist. Since this was just before the 56th anniversary of the main German offensive on Verdun on 21 February 1917, speculations immediately arose that the motive for the *commando* raid – all the more sensational because it took place under the nose of a Police Post 500 metres from the gravesite – was both a political-historical statement and an attempt to reinter Pétain's remains at Douaumont. In fact, his former lawyer Jacques Isnori, who had long been calling for the official *translation* of Pétain's ashes from Île d'Yeu to Douaumont, but who also *grandly condemned* the coffin's hijack, received an anonymous phone call suggesting that the popular supposition was well founded.

On Île d'Yeu, Jean Taraud explained to the press the technique two or three men would have used to remove the 650 kg tombstone, using a chisel and a crowbar. The newspapers sifted other stories of a foreign yacht in the harbor, a helicopter flying over the island at 4 am and apparent arrivals and departures of light aircraft. A blue van that arrived on the ferry from Fromentine on the previous Saturday and left on the Monday morning was noted. Apparently, the van carried woollen goods and a woman associated with it had registered at *la mairie* to open a stall at the market. Remarkably, her name was Mademoiselle Boche. Some stories contrasted the indignation of the older generation with the astonished fascination of the younger one.

On Tuesday 20 February, the situation in the snow around Verdun was tense. On one side, a national police dragnet paid special attention to routes – particularly small tracks – into the Ossuary at Douaumont. The police also consulted clairvoyants to inquire into the possibility that the body had already been reinterred. On the other side, veterans waited *feverishly* in a heavy fog at Verdun for the return of their leader, while the departmental president Monsieur Vincent said he was ready *to assist the men who had transferred the body ... and I will not be the only one.* The bishop of Verdun Monsignor Boillon indicated that he would be another.

Wednesday 21 February: Prime Minister Pierre Messmer held fast to the official line. *Beyond any historical or political problem*, he said, *the majority of French people find themselves confronted with proceedings that, on the moral plane, are particularly odious.*

The break-through came in Paris. This followed investigations involving *one van with two registration numbers.* Other factors were the interrogation of a number of individuals, including a 60-year-old Paris garage owner with a stolen identity card and one 38-year-old Mademoiselle Solange Boche from Etrechy (Essonne), who cracked under protracted questioning. Then, *the chief of the commando*, 35-year-old Algerian War veteran and 19th arrondissement candidate for the legislative elections Hubert Massol gave a sensational press conference. Presenting himself as a member of the Executive Bureau of the Republican Alliance, he announced that the intention was indeed the rehabilitation and deposition of Pétain's remains at Douaumont and that *If I am arrested, no one will find the body*. He was immediately arrested. The blue van was found abandoned near the Eiffel Tower and the body was retrieved from beneath a pile of mattresses in the Paris garage of the interrogated owner.

Thursday 22 February: the sun was shining for the second funeral, as it was for the first. The body was returned to the island by Puma helicopter at 11.37 am (seven minutes ahead of schedule) and, after a long funeral procession through the villages, a good-natured crowd of young and old gathered around the grave at 2.30 pm.

The handful of remaining Île d'Yeu 1914-18 veterans mounted a *moving* guard of honour. (This group had in fact been divided over Pétain until de Gaulle's wreath in 1968 initiated their reconciliation.) Pétain's great nephew and the former head of his Civil Cabinet Louis-Dominique Girard was the only family member present. A Presidential wreath was one of only four; the others were from the family, the local commune, and the Pétain-Verdun association, which attached an emblem emblazoned with the conciliatory words *Honour and Pardon*. Beside the tomb, Pétain's old confessor Abbé Germain Pontheau, now 75, said a last prayer, offered incense and gave the benediction, which was drowned out by the chatter of the onlookers and the sound of a light aircraft flying overhead. The ceremony was over in five minutes.

The greatest heat generated by the affair seems to have come from within the Pétain family itself. Girard, who attended the second funeral, took the same view as Isnori: it was preferable to acknowledge the burial on Île d'Yeu as a stage in the final rehabilitation and burial of the remains at Douaumont. However, the Marshal's niece Madame Berthe Pétain came out saying that, *for her part, she would have preferred that the coffin be sent straight to Douaumont.* The widow of the Marshal's son-in-law Madame François de Herain took a more nuanced position: *if it were not possible to bury the coffin at Douaumont, and if the government had consulted me, I would have asked that he rest in the family crypt at Montparnasse Cemetery. In that crypt there is a free space beside his wife. That would have been a step towards something less ugly.* However, when Madame de Herain took out writs against those who had *profaned the tomb,* yet another branch, that of the du Tertre family from the Nantes region, came out in strong opposition against her. Since the grandmother of Madame de Herain's husband was numbered among the du Tertres, this branch felt it had *at least as great a moral right over the memory of Marshal Pétain as Madame de Herain.* That branch also applauded the *chivalrous gesture* of those who had wanted the last wishes of the victor of Verdun to be respected.

In broad terms, the political passion surrounding Pétain was in the past. What *Ouest France* described as this *rocambolesque* affair had turned out to be a national entertainment, which nonetheless incited some serious reflection. On 23 February, for example, the same journal contained an article on the new documentary *film-fleuve* in three, three-hour episodes, *Français, si vous saviez* by André Harris and Alain de Sedouy. These film makers had worked on the celebrated Marcel Ophüls documentary *Le chagrin et le pitié* about France under the German occupation. The *film-fleuve* had now gone on to document the story from Pétain to de Gaulle by focusing on three moments ranging across 50 years: the defeat in 1940, the re-surfacing of a battered France in 1944, and the passing of the Republic in 1958. The point here, however, is that, before the lifting of Pétain's coffin, the documentary had been approved for release in Paris on the same afternoon as his second funeral. A film, which seemed far removed from current events, unexpectedly found itself at the heart of them.

One long-term beneficiary of Pétain's macabre legacy is worth noting. Standard references in Île d'Yeu travel brochures show that, today, although not outshining the Old Château, his tomb is one of the island's top tourist attractions.

VII

We are not exactly tourists; we are visitors accompanying friends from the Turbé family, which has a long history on the island. (*Petite histoire* mentions, for example, that in 1808 the mayor was a Monsieur Célestin Turbé.) And our friendship means that we are now looking into the future over the vacant block of land in Port Joinville to which we have just driven from the dense enclosure of Fort de Pierre Levée.

Since their children have left home, Dominique and Dominique have sold the house at Sautron, near Nantes. They rented the old one at Le Temple and bought the land we are now surveying. They are planning to acquire an apartment in Nantes and build a house on Île d'Yeu. Still with a place in town, Dominique will be close to where he came from. Dominique, who comes from Normandy, also wants to live on the island, although at Port Joinville, because, as she said during the squall this morning, living elsewhere would be far too isolated in winter. A tree line runs along the back of the block; sturdy white houses stand on either side of it. Although freestanding, these houses still evoke cabins on a white ship. They are indicative of how the Dominiques will fill the space between them.

We have circumnavigated the island. Back at the port, the colours have cooled in the late afternoon light. In the distance, a bluer palette overshadows the dazzling morning one, picking up on the sky and water and engaging with different shades of white. Dominique returns the jeep. Dominique, Monique, and Edith do some shopping; they are looking at vests in what was probably an old boat shed now turned into a tourist shop. I sit nearby on a seriously worn, cement-rendered brick fence looking around the harbour, waiting to catch the ferry.

Coming to me on the water, is the way one of Napoleon's officials described Île d'Yeu; *as a lone ship floating on the sea.* In his day, the weather or else British warships could cut the island off from the continent for six weeks. Monsieur Esseul explains that in periods when the postal boat came from the port at Saint-Gilles with its open heads, rather than from the more sheltered anchorage at Fromentine, connections could still break down for long spells. Heavy seas could close Saint-Gilles for days or, even, weeks, thus severing Port Joinville's links with the outside world.

Even in 1945, when it took the French navy well over two hours to transport Pétain from La Pallice to Port Joinville, his exile there showed that Île d'Yeu was still widely thought to be an isolated place. Since then, much has changed. A pipeline carrying the island's water connects it permanently with the continent. Access by air takes a few minutes. When the ferry carries us back to Fromentine, it will take less than three-quarters of an hour. Such proximity promotes economic integration with the continent. As a result, EEC quotas threaten the fishing industry and tourism may have greater power than all earlier invasions to reshape the way of life.

Technology does not change everything. The

islanders have their own topography, beaches, microclimates, flowers, colour schemes, songs, and stories. I will learn that Maurice Esseul passed away on 7 May 2021. Yet the islanders still have their own historian, one who has dedicated to me *notre passionnante histoire insulaire*, our captivating island history, in the beautifully handwritten inscription he has made in my copy of his book. As long as the limitless reaches of sky and ocean remain the measure of the islanders' small landmass, they will also have a truly global outlook. Île d'Yeu is still an island with an ancient identity floating on the sea.

We take the ferry back to Fromentine and pick up the land cruiser. The return trip to Le Temple takes us back through the Vendée, where a thin black line of traffic wends its way along a narrow road between flat, straw-coloured fields for as far as the eye can see. Later we pass through villages that face right onto the road. This is not the new world built in large measure around the automobile. This is the automobile fitting into a world that was still, not much more than a century ago, laced together with bullock cart tracks.

The house at Le Temple is not far past the church corner and faces right onto the road. We unpack the car and go inside to get ready for dinner. My copy of *Pilote de guerre* is sitting on a small table in the dining room. After looking through the book the other night and reading the passages Claude had marked, I returned it to Dominique saying that he could not give me such a gift without an inscription from him. He had taken the book away and, apparently, having written something in it, placed it on the table for me to collect.

On the page inside the cover, Dominique has written a dedication that, to my astonishment, embodies the arch of the world:

> *À mon cher ami Greg,*
> *De la petite île d'Yeu à la grande île d'Australie*
> *C'était le destin de ce livre*
> *L'amitié est un bien précieux*

> To my dear friend Greg,
> From the small île d'Yeu to the
> large island of Australia
> That was the destiny of this book
> Friendship is a precious possession.

Acknowledgements

No one has been more central to the weaving of my worlds and histories than my wife Monique. We met at Sydney University in the shadow of the fall of Saigon. We married in love and expectation of a future, from which the ruins of the past would forever recede. Much of my writing since then has been about reaching into the past to find hope for the future.

Going to France was a crucial part of that enterprise. Going to postwar Vietnam much later was too. Focused by our friendship with Dominique and Dominique Turbé and, also, by various exigencies of my work, which included not being able to get a visa to conduct research in post-war Vietnam until 1989, however, the small island on which I found my post-war global memory was French. My readings of Maurice Esseul's *Petite histoire de l'île d'Yeu* (and of some email correspondence we had) were then indispensable to my understanding of the place.

The moment I learnt we were going to visit Île d'Yeu, I knew I had a story. I don't fully understand that intuition, but feel it was inseparable from my anticipation of the intersecting narratives that awaited me there.

When, in 2012, I returned to the large island of Australia and wrote the story, I had no literary models in mind. Intensified by my short, sharp interaction with the island and its history, however, my inclination was to write a story that was out of sync, although not at odds with the objectivity so rigorously demanded by my historical training. My impulse was to subjectify history, not in some populist disregard for objective truth and reality, but with greater self-awareness of their vital importance in relating it.

The story of my visit to the island seemed to be inseparable from the other histories that had propelled me to it and engaged me there: most immediately my Vietnam War histories. Though apparently remote from those, the ones I found important to me there had to be interconnected with them in my self-awareness.

I was decentring the histories that seemed important to me – as they had indeed decentred *me*. And while I was unaware of influences for this while writing, that did not mean there were none.

There were, I now think, two influences: the German writer W.G. Sebald and the French historian Pierre Nora. Without the advice of leading Australian intellectual and cultural historian John Docker, it is also the case that I may never have realised the influence of either.

John introduced me to Nora's work around 2015 and later used Nora's term *ego-histoire* to describe the landmark three-volume Australian autobiography he was then working on: *Growing up Communist and Jewish in Bondi* (2020). The excellent Preface and Introduction to that exceptional work also discusses Nora's essay 'L'ego-histoire est-elle possible?', 'Is ego-history possible?'.

The preliminary definition of Nora's *ego-histoire*

idea, which John offers in the Prologue to his work, is entirely straight forward: *family histories that intersect with wider histories.* My variation on that definition would merely be to specify *individual histories* as well as the *family histories,* which intersect with the wider ones. When John eventually read my story, written with no knowledge of Nora's thinking, he said it *does indeed resonate with Pierre Nora's notions of ego-histoire.*

The *I* in Nora's *ego-histoire* is not self-centred; it is rather pushed off balance in the ego historian's identification with others. As the wider histories, which are often related in different genres, crowd around demanding consideration, the literary problem of achieving narrative balance becomes paramount. *The texts the ego historian produces are always close to vertigo,* John writes following Nora. *Genre in ego histoire tosses about like a drunken boat* – the *bateau ivre* metaphor, which goes back in French culture to the 1871 poem of that name by Jean-Nicholas-Arthur Rimbaud, and which happened to be in vogue among Australian and New Zealand writers in the 1960s and beyond.

The issue of narrative balance certainly presented in my story. Seemingly remote or dissimilar events and texts kept popping up between private memory, or what's left of it, and collective history. On visiting the Old Château in Part One, for example, my response was to connect with its history through disparate others that made sense to me: Froissart's fifteenth century *Chronicles*, 1950s Kurosawa films, and my own history. Hence, the potential for all kinds of narrative connections to pile up and, as Nora realised, to threaten something like a dizzying sensation of being tossed around in a story with no bottom – or top. And hence the key literary demand for a definition of the narrative core, a narrative imperative that might be expressed as a need for the literary alignment of the story's historical content with the personalised subjectivity of its beginning and end.

I mentioned W.G. Sebald. This is because I feel, in retrospect, that his fictional prose narratives had influenced me by making their subjectivity a plausible measure of objective history and vice-versa.

Sebald's literary response to the monstrous legacy of his generation had seemed incomparable to me in its comprehensiveness and humility. The four prose narratives in his second book *The Emigrants* (1993 in German, 1996 in English), which first came my way, seemed to be pitched with such desolate beauty and vulnerability over the dark abyss of human chaos that it forever threatens to claim not only their subjects, but the narratives themselves. Inherent in those stories, the tragic, overarching sense of loss seemed to be the key to their completeness.

Still, Sebald's writing was not high in my mind when I wrote in 2012. At that time, my narrative merely mentioned in passing the title of his scholarly essay 'Air War and Literature'. He was not an historian, and, in any case, I never felt I had been born into the state of total moral as well as political and cultural collapse from which his writing may be seen to arise.

A strong sense of duty and, I believe, moral responsibility had shielded me in Vietnam. I was shocked when Saigon fell in 1975. When I left the army, it never occurred to me to repudiate my experience. Australia was also far from moral or cultural collapse at the time. I found myself supported by many institutions. These were the University of

Sydney, where I studied; the Australian National University, where I worked; the Vietnam Veterans' Federation of Australia, of which I was a member and honorary historian; and, at one point, the Army itself, which provided a grant that helped me finish my 2007 book *The Minefield*. I had been able to pursue outside the army, the historical questions raised by my experience inside it. What had been the nature of the war that revealed so resoundingly the irrelevance of Australian strategic policy in relation to it? How then had Australian forces fared in the strategic incoherence they faced in Vietnam?

Compared with Sebald's preoccupations, these seemed to be narrowly strategic and reinforced by my historical, not to mention military, cladding. But while dutifully and, I again believe, morally banishing *self-awareness* from *my* objective histories – a theoretical impossibility if the truth be teased out – those works inevitably engaged *me* in the construction of a post-colonial or, if one prefers today, a post-colonising Australian narrative that had a subjective dimension. I think that reading Sebald had left me with related inklings about the possibility of making that dimension explicit in an historical narrative.

How might Sebald's writing have influenced me?

Writing in Gerhard Fischer's edited bilingual volume *W.G. Sebald* (2009), Lynn Wolff quotes a comment Sebald once made about his own writing. It was *all about the millions that were sent to the gas chambers,* he said, *but these were not anonymous masses; they were always individual human beings who had actually lived on the other side of the corridor.* Wolff also quotes a related comment that Sebald had made in his posthumous volume *Campo Santo* (English, 2005), one that I had been unable to forget after I first read it there. Reflecting on the kind of writing that might be commensurable with the catastrophic loss of millions of the individuals he believed his work was about, Sebald said: *there are many forms of writing; only in literature, however, can there be an attempt at restitution over and above the mere recital of facts, and over and above scholarship.* For me, Sebald's conception of *literature* lies between those quotes.

By *literature* he did not necessarily mean works of fiction – novels. He stressed he was an author of *prose narratives*, even though they were fictional. Yet, he also stressed the importance of documented history, and his *prose narratives* have a definite *documentary* element. They include historical detail. Some of his photographs are also documentary. As many have realised, his writing problematises the boundary between history and fiction, leaving the issue of genre in his *prose narratives* unresolved.

This essential uncertainty in Sebald's work brings one to the problem or, even more, to *the impossibility* of representing historical modernity, particularly its signature events. By any reckoning these would include the Nazi holocaust, which interested him, and the *American War* in Indochina, which embraced no *final solution* but killed comparable numbers of people – some five million locals at the high end of the range, plus Americans, Australians, and others – which interests me. As writers and artists have long realised, such overwhelming losses amplify the impossibility of representation.

Enter, as Wolff realises, Sebald's literary distrust of language. By way of illustration, she mentions Austerlitz, the protagonist in Sebald's book of the same name, *Austerlitz* (2001), who uses rich figurative language to *express his deception by lan-*

guage and the elusiveness of meaning. So elusive are Sebald's circuitous prose narratives that, indeed, we may underline an often-remarked aspect of them: they avoid naming the event that gave rise to and looms over them.

Something else Wolff's says fits that narrative subtlety. Since the holocaust, she stresses, the impossibility of representation has required writers *to get beyond fixing an image, a memory, or a narrative.* Amplifying Sebald's approach to memory, or, let us say, to unfixing it, she concludes that his writing had reconceptualised it *more as a process ... than as something one possesses ...* .[6] For him memory is more a reconstruction than a revival or replay.

Either way, of course, memory, which has primacy in *all* storytelling, history, or fiction, arises from self-awareness, which involves the *I* as an analogue of the so-called real world, but which is also subjective. Does not the special, often painful salience of the reconstructed subjectivity in Sebald's elusive accounts then come into its own? Is

---

6. Wolff further suggests, astutely in my view, an argument that Sebald is creating a poetics of transitive memory in order to deconstruct the notion of memory as a thing to be possessed in a subject-object relationship with the individual. Also see Rachel Aviv, 'How Elizabeth Loftus Changed the Meaning of Memory', The New Yorker, March 29, 2021.

this not what has constituted his attempt to restore in the collective (particularly German) imagination a place for all those who had disappeared from it during the holocaust? As I take it, that salience of subjectivity in his reconstruction of both historical and fictional memory – in his prose narratives – constituted his *attempt at restitution.*

That is why I think his work had attuned me to an elemental aspect of literature that, for all its virtues, academic historiography side-lines. Close to the reference John Docker makes in the Preface of his *ego-histoire* to Rimbaud, we are in the zone of that poet's celebrated formulation *Je est un autre*, I is someone else. Sebald's work had drawn out my related assurance that *I is in my objective history.*

As indicated, absorbing Sebald's prose narratives had also meant absorbing indirectly something unknown to me until talking to John in 2015: the influence of Nora's work itself. Long again, indeed, after John's introduction to Nora, Gerhard told me about Sebald's interest in Nora's *lieux de mémoire,* sites of memory — monuments, museums, buildings, old coins, and artefacts — and in his *ego-histoire.*

Suddenly, I had an expanded understanding of why Sebald's first book was called *Vertigo* (1990). More ample comprehension also seemed to get through to me of the vertiginous note on which the Ambrose Adelwarth story in *The Emigrants* so explicitly ends: *Memory ... often strikes me as a kind of dumbness. It makes one's head heavy and giddy, as if one were not looking back down the receding perspectives of time but rather down on the earth from a great height, from one of those towers whose tops are lost to view in the clouds.* For me, the rather overwhelming vertical axis in Seblad's prose narraives had implied a limitless pile of stories, as a precondition of what Nora had called *ego-histoire*.

On the horizontal plane, his main prose narratives also open wide geographical spaces. *The Emigrants* connects Europe with Britain and the United States. *The Rings of Saturn* (German 1995, English 1998) is written around a walk in the English countryside. *Austerlitz* (German and English, 2001) spans Britain and Europe; it also visits Africa and Indonesia. As it happens, the *lieux de mémoire,* which present across these spaces, have as much to do with bodies and human remains as they do with lost eras; they include crumbling cemeteries, modern construction sites that have broken into the graves of the dead, art representing bodies or forgotten diaries full of lost worlds, even rocks and natural features, all of which provoke contemplation of the history of natural and man-made destruction.

Resurrected complexly from the bed of especially man-made catastrophe – strewn with bodies and bones – Sebald's characters embody his attempted literary mission: restitution in remembrance of all those lost in the holocaust. And indeed, for me, his characters are so finely, yet firmly formed in the history of that event they become literary *archetypes* which speak, feel, and act for all its victims. The potential for a vertical ascent into the possibility of endless stories piling up around the dizzied author is implicit – as it would be in *ego-histoire*.[7]

---

7. The culminating *lieu de mémoire* in Sebald's last complete prose narrative *Austerlitz* could hardly be more dizzying – especially when in architectural reality it was grounded in something that has also been described as *un trou de mémoire*, a hole in the collective consciousness of the German occupation of Paris.

Jacques Austerlitz, an architectural historian, had grown up in Wales after his parents sent him away from Prague for his own safety on a *child transport* in late 1939. In Wales, his Calvinist foster parents had erased his former identity, and so he is searching for clues of his lost parents and irrecoverable past. Set within the wider man-made ecological as well as material catastrophes in Sebald's work, which Gerhard's analysis stresses with sharp insight, an unusually capacious account of the holocaust comes out.

There are holocausts and holocausts, although perhaps none more evil than the Nazi German one. In any case, I've come to think that a metanarrative of individual or family sensibility, which arose from the giddying stories of lost multitudes and their histories, was the object of my great early admiration for Sebald's writing. Without me realising it, Sebald's books had attuned me to the possibility

---

The vertical literary layering already inherent in Austerlitz's own narrative of suppressed memory occurs in the somber psychological space of his search for himself across Britain and Europe. Therein, the oblique, subtly depressive voice of the narrator wends its way in and out and around the railway stations and shunting yards, the cemeteries and violated graves, and, of course, the *star-shaped* military fortifications that go back to Vauban and constitute the central metaphor of the story. Not long before the end, when *Austerlitz* is searching for traces of his father in Paris, we then visit the climactic site: the Babylonian towers of France's new Bibliothèque Nationale, which was opened in 1996, a monument to the French President, at Tolbiac.

In a giddying redefinition of how a library aspires to house *the memory of the world*, the towers of glass and steel soar into the sky. But, as Austerlitz conducts his fictional research in those spires, he learns from a fictional librarian named Henri Lemoine something of real moral and cultural significance. The towers are built on platforms, which cover a virtually forgotten historical site near the Gare d'Austerlitz on the Paris *Métro*. This is the *Métro* stop, after which the site took its name, and after which Sebald named his book, on finding out about it, probably around 1997 from scattered pieces in the Jewish press in Paris.

Sebald was in fact writing about the former Camp Austerlitz and large storehouse complex, in which Jewish prisoners had processed the loot the Nazis had plundered from what appears to have been some 38,000 Jewish apartments in the city during the war. Sebald's revelation that a great monument of French culture stood on the forgotten site of such a crime against humanity was quickly followed up. In another excellent contribution to Gerhard's volume, James L. Cowan's essay studies what was known about the camp and says that, within a year of the 2002 publication of the French translation of Sebald's book, Jean-Marc Dreyfus and Sarah Gensburger had produced the key work: *Des camps dans Paris: Austerlitz, Levitan, Bassano, juillet 1943 — août 1944* (2003). This was indeed the work, which perceived the *trou de mémoire* in the collective awareness of those dark days and, also, credited Sebald's book for helping to bring it to light.

Meanwhile, back in the book, Austerlitz loses his father's trail. The narrative shifts from Paris to the former Nazi fortress at Breendonk near Antwerp around where the story started and where it is, in the end, extinguished. One might perhaps think that we have an attempted *ego-histoire* of Austerlitz – or of the narrator or both – that because of lost memory can never become one in either fiction or history.

of writing a narrative that, indeed, resonates with Nora's idea of *ego-histoire* – of putting *my history in the histories of others or of recovering it through them.*

Those histories of others, to which that day on Île d'Yeu happened to connect me, were those that got me to Vietnam in the first place. As Vietnam got me to France and France to the island, its history was the one wherein I finally assembled my own past, as I had formerly put together my post-Vietnam war histories, in a post-colonial perspective — after considerable reading in the beautiful reading room of France's old Bibliothèque Nationale in Rue de Richelieu, Paris.

At the time of writing in 2012 my friend for two-thirds of a lifetime, Bruce Pollard owner of Pinacotheca Gallery, as important as any in modern Australian art history, helped me get to where I was going, anyway. As did another, whose friendship and advice have long endured, combat officer and leading advocate for veterans' welfare Graham Walker. Another long-term friend who has enriched my life and writing – in this book as elsewhere – with his readiness to listen and offer critical advice is Trevor Fuller, an engineer, who is deeply interested in the arts. I owe a similar debt to historian Professor David Walker, whose books on Asian influences in Australian culture and memoirs help lead us into the future.

Four old classmates since Duntroon days have at different times also read and commented generously on the manuscript: Ross Sydney, Kevin O'Brien, Peter Rose, and Graham Edney. Another friend from a senior class at Duntroon, John Hopman, did the same.

No false friends or easy readers either, Douglas Newton, Val Noone, and Jim Gerrand, who all read the early manuscript, commented, and encouraged me to publish it. I have mentioned more than once John Docker and Professor Gerhard Fischer and further value Professor Margaret Sankey's reading and advice during the early stages of the work. Thanks to Darren Mitchell, who recently read the manuscript twice for content and read it again to help root out typos, and to Martin Edmond, for his two readings of the manuscript and fine editorial advice. Thanks also to Michele Fuller, who twice read with care and a sharp eye the manuscript at a late stage. While none of these people are responsible for my shortcomings, I am gratefully indebted to them all.

The beginning of a story is rightfully in the end, as the end is in the beginning. Therefore, I should say finally that my wife Monique and our friends Dominique and Dominique Turbé read the manuscript in 2021, as they did in 2012, and end on the point that without them this story would not exist.

Bibliography

Aviv, Rachel, 'How Elizabeth Loftus Changed the Meaning of Memory', *The New Yorker*, March 29, 2021.

Bemelmans, Ludwig, 'The Island of God', *The New Yorker*, 5 August 1939, reissued 28 June and 13 October 2021.

Bloomsbury, *The New Yorker Book of War Pieces: London 1939-Hiroshima 1945*, London, 1989, Paperback, 1990.

Brickhill, Paul, *The Great Escape*, Faber, London, 1950

Brickhill, Paul, *The Dambusters*, Evan Brothers, London,1951; Pan 1954.

Brickhill, Paul, *Reach for the Sky*, Collins, London, 1954.

Caesar, Ed,'Underworld', *The New Yorker, July 27, 2020*.

Céline, Louis-Ferdinand, *D'un château l'autre* (Castle to Castle), Gallimard, Paris, 1957.

Céline, Louis-Ferdinand, *Castle to Castle*, translated from the French by Ralph Manheim, Dalkey Archive Press, 2011.

Dreyfus, Jean-Marc and Sarah Gensburger, *Des camps dans Paris: Austerlitz, Levitan, Bassano, juillet 1943 — août 1944 (The camps in Paris: Austerlitz, Levitan, Bassano, july 1943 — august 1944)*, FAYARD Editions, Paris, 2003.

Esseul, Maurice, *Petite histoire de l'île d'Yeu* (A Short History of Île d'Yeu), Geste éditions, La Crèche, 2012.

Gerber, François, *Saint-Exupéry, écrivain en guerre* (Saint-Exupéry, a writer at war), Éditions Jacob-Duvernet, Paris, 2012.

Fischer, Gerhard, *Enemy Aliens: internment and the homefront experience in Australia 1914-1920*, University of Queensland Press, Brisbane, 1989.

Fischer, Gerhard, ed., *W.G. Sebald: Schreiben ex patria/Expatriate Writing*, Rodopi, Amsterdam, New York, 2009.

Fischer, Gerhard, 'Zur politischen Ästhetik einer Holocaust-Literatur. W.G. Sebalds Prosabuch *Austerlitz*' ('On the political aesthetics of a Holocaust-Literature: W.G. Sebald's Prose Book *Austerlitz*.') In: *Politische Literatur: Debatten, Begriffe, Aktualität*, eds. Christine Lubkoll, Manuel Illi, Anna Hampe, Stuttgart: Metzler, 2018, 251–268.

Knoke, Heinz, *I Flew for the Fuhrer: The Story of a German Airman*, first English edition, 1953, Greenhill Books, London, 2020.

Kuncz, Aladár, *Black Monastery*, translated from the original Hungarian, *A FEKETE KOLOSTOR*, 1931, by Ralph Harry, Chatto and Windus, London, 1934.

Kuncz, Aladár,, *Le Monastère noir* (Black Monastery), Gallimard, Paris, 1937; L'Étrave, Beauvois-sur-mer, Vendée, 1999, 2014.

Loti, Pierre, *Pêcheur d'Islande* (An Iceland Fisherman), originally 1886, Le Livre de Poche, 1988.

Martyn, Errol W., *For your tomorrow – a Record of New Zealanders who have died while serving with the RNZAF and Allied Air Services since 1915*, three volumes, Volplane Press, New Zealand, 1998

Martyn, Errol W., *Swift to the Sky: New Zealand's Military Aviation History*, Penguin/Viking, 2010.

Massonie, Albert, *J'ai soigné Pétain* (I treated Pétain), Tallandier, Paris, 2017.

Muller, Jean-Léon, 'Une mémoire hongroise particulière: le cas d'Aladár Kuncz', *Guerres mondiales et conflits contemporains*, ('A special Hungarian memoir: the case of Aladár Kuncz', *World Wars and Contemporary Conflicts*, 2007/4, number 228, pp. 81-89.

Nora, Pierre, 'Between Memory and History: *Les Lieux de Mémoire*,' translated by Marc Roudebush, *Representations*, No. 26 Special Issue: Memory and Counter-Memory, University of California Press, (Spring 1989), 7-24.

Paxton, Robert, *Vichy France: Old Guard and New Order, 1940-1944*, originally Knopf, New York, Columbia University Press, New York, 1972, 2001.

Saki, Saburo with Martin Caidin and Fred Saito, *Samurai*, E.P. Dutton, Boston, 1957.

de Saint-Exupéry, Antoine, *Vol de nuit (Night Flight)*, Gallimard, Paris, 1931.

de Saint-Exupéry, Antoine, *Pilote de guerre* (Flight to Arras), Gallimard, Paris, originally 1942, 1943.

de Saint-Exupéry, Antoine, *Flight to Arras*, translated by Lewis Galantière, Reynal and Hitchcock, New York, 1942; Penguin, 1961.

de Saint-Exupéry, Antoine, *Lettre A Un Otage* (Letter to a Hostage), Gallimard, Paris, 1944.

de Saint-Exupéry, Antoine, *Le Petit Prince* (The Little Prince), Gallimard, 1946.

Ouest France (West France), La Vendée, 20-23 February 1973 for articles on the heist of Pétin's coffin and his 'second funeral'.

Schama, Simon, *A History of Britain: At the Edge of the World? 3000BC – AD 1603*, BBC, London, 2000.

Schiff, Stacy, *Saint-Exupéry, a biography*, Henry Holt and Company, New York, 2006.

Sebald, W.G., *Vertigo*, translated by Michael Hulse, Harvill Press, London, 1996.

Sebald, W.G., *The Emigrants*, translated by Michael Hulse, Harvill, London, 1996.

Sebald, W.G., *Austerlitz*, translated by Anthea Bell, Hamish Hamilton, London, 2001.

Sebald, W.G., 'Air War and Literature': Zürich Lectures', in *On the Natural History of Destruction*, translated by Anthea Bell, Hamish Hamilton, London, 2003.

Sebald, W.G., *Campo Santo*, edited by Sven Myer, translated by Anthea Bell, Hamish Hamilton, London, 2005.

Williams, Charles, *Pétain*, Little, Brown, London, 2005.

Greg Lockhart was born in 1947 at Monto in Queensland and grew up on the Illawarra Coast of New South Wales. A graduate of Duntroon, the Royal Military College of Australia, he served with the Pacific Islands Regiment in Papua New Guinea and with the Australian Army in the Vietnam War. After leaving the Army in 1975, he took BA (Honours I) and PhD Degrees in History from the University of Sydney and worked at the Australian National University. He is author of *Nation in Arms: the origins of the People's Army of Vietnam* (1989), *The Minefield: An Australian tragedy in Vietnam* (2007) and others, including his co-translation with his wife Monique of three modern Vietnamese classics in *The Light of the Capital* (1996). He lives in Sydney and is Honorary Historian of the Vietnam Veterans' Federation of Australia.

www.ingramcontent.com/pod-product-compliance
Lightning Source LLC
Chambersburg PA
CBHW020323010526
44107CB00054B/1961